The Crusades and Silk Road

A Captivating Guide to Religious Wars During the Middle Ages and an Ancient Network of Trade Routes

Free Bonus from Captivating History (Available for a Limited time)

Hi History Lovers!

Now you have a chance to join our exclusive history list so you can get your first history ebook for free as well as discounts and a potential to get more history books for free! Simply visit the link below to join.

Captivatinghistory.com/ebook

Also, make sure to follow us on Facebook, Twitter and Youtube by searching for Captivating History.

Contents

An Introduction to the Crusades and Silk Road

Contact between Europe and China developed slowly over many centuries. From a Western viewpoint, it spanned the era from the fall of Rome to the beginning of the Renaissance around 1400. During the Age of Discovery, European seafarers burst out of the Mediterranean and sought a sea route to India, where highly prized spices could be acquired. They soon pushed east from India, and maritime trade expanded into Southeast Asia and to China itself. This efficient mode of trade ended interest in finding the overland route between Europe and China.

The history of overland commerce between the two ends of the then known world is seen as a side effect of the period of the Crusades, at least from the European perspective. In the era of knightly fighting in the Holy Land and adjacent lands, Europeans came to learn about the cultures of the Near East and beyond. Before the Crusades, Europeans were disinclined to push trade and exploration beyond the coast of the Mediterranean in the East because of the presence of hostile Muslims and disinterest in what lay in the interior of Asia. The Europeans' ignorance of that half of the world, beyond the frontiers of the Holy Land, slowly remedied over several centuries.

Overland contact with the West by the Chinese developed equally slowly. Because of their system of centralized government and the pragmatic way in which the Chinese expanded trade westward into Central Asia, there was no pressing motive for them to hasten to the far reaches of the globe in search of goods or wealth that they didn't already have.

To fully understand how the Silk Road became an exotic concept in the West and how the many archaeological sites along this route have become powerful magnets for modern tourists, it is necessary to understand how this route became a melting pot for various cultures and how it was transformed into a safe passage for traders and explorers who traveled it.

Firstly, the designation of the overland trade route between Europe and China is fraught with confusion. When the term "the Silk Road" was invented in the last quarter of the 19th century, it was taken to mean a single trade highway, along which goods and ideas were transmitted between Europe and China and vice versa. After meticulous research on archaeological remains and ancient texts, it has become clear that merchants in the centuries following the collapse of the Western Roman Empire in the 4th century CE traded with merchants during the rise of dynastic China. However, this trade was conducted over a series of short paths instead of one lengthy highway. In fact, very few of these goods actually made the complete journey from China to Europe.

The term "the Silk Road" is still used today among scholars studying modern and contemporary economics around the transfer of goods from the Far East to Europe, North and South America, and Africa. There is nothing mysteriously romantic about the Silk Road as it is understood and used by contemporary economists. What they mean by the term today is unclear. Certainly, this trade has almost nothing to do with silk, and it is not land-based as we understand the word "road" to mean. Generally, the Silk Road, as used in modern-day economics, refers to the routes that are used to exchange goods originating in the East and in the West. To further complicate the issue, we now understand trade to include services, primarily digital, that are geographically synchronous. In one sense then, the digital highway may be considered a new route of the Silk Road.

The explosion of global consumption of goods and services was brought on by the so-called consumer revolution. The impact of consumerism and trade on regional economies has led economists to adopt the term "the Silk Road." They use this term metaphorically, resurrecting the model of medieval trade between Europe and what is now modern-day China. The historical Silk Road was something quite unlike what modern economists would have us believe it once was.

Substantial trade between Europe and China was something that was very slow to develop. Geography, cultural psychology, and social conditions in both the East and the West hindered contact between the two "worlds." In the period of the Han dynasty (202 BCE–220 CE), Chinese influence expanded into Central Asia. But this expansion was tenuous at best. Local tribes and cultures constantly revolted against the Chinese administrations. Central Asia was wilder in terms of intertribal conflict than the peaceful (albeit intermittent) Chinese control. Trade beyond the borders of Han China was a risky undertaking at best.

In the West, following the reign of Alexander the Great of Macedonia (r. 336–323 BCE), who had pushed his empire into Central Asia, the Romans made occasional contact with Asian traders operating in the Near East. These traders offered goods they, in turn, had acquired from Central Asian merchants. It is possible that some of the Central Asian merchants may have come all the way from China. If the discovery of Roman coinage is an indication of trade, then the Romans had economic connections with marine traders around the Indian Ocean but not with any land-locked cultures beyond Afghanistan. The possibility that the Romans acquired luxury goods such as Chinese silk from Central Asian traders is not borne out by archaeological research. There is an absence of objects in Roman sites that could have come from as far away as China.

Although it is a misnomer to call the routes from India up through Afghanistan to Central Asia "the Silk Road," the terminology persists. Along this route, substantial exchanges of goods and ideas occurred from very early times. It was along the route that Buddhism was transmitted from its original home in India up through Central Asia and on into China. Buddhist texts were translated from Sanskrit into Chinese in the early 5th century CE.

In Europe, as the central, organized administration of the Roman Empire crumbled, tribes, which were now unrestrained, migrated from beyond the unguarded frontiers of the Roman Empire. As a result, interest in trade in the eastern Mediterranean declined. The Roman seaborne trade economy diminished. From the 5th century to the 8th century, any designs Europeans might have on trade or conquests in the Levant were held in check. This was partly due to the presence of a rival Christian Byzantine Empire in Constantinople (modern-day Istanbul), which claimed sole authority to expand eastward. In the eastern Mediterranean, traders of the East Roman Empire, also known as the Byzantine Empire, held sway. There is little evidence to suggest that Byzantine merchants pushed much beyond the accessible coastal regions.

As the Western Roman Empire began to collapse in the 4th century CE, several nomadic tribes shoved their way into and through Europe in a period that is called the Dark Ages. They invaded the remnants of the Roman Empire, pillaging their way through the lands. Over time, these tribes adopted a settled life and amalgamated with the peoples of pre-existing cultures in the conquered territories. Tribal cultures slowly evolved into organized societies, somewhat like modern-day states. Kingdoms and empires, like the Carolingian Empire (800 CE–888 CE) and the Ottonian dynasty (919 CE–1024 CE), rose and fell, as did the influence of the Christian Church, which was under the administration of the pope in Rome. Tribal languages evolved into vernacular tongues. Some were influenced by Latin, such as Italian and French, while others, such as Old Norse, German, Dutch, and English, evolved from Indo-European languages. Official communication throughout Europe was accomplished through Latin, which was the language of the Western Christian Church centered in Rome and the vestigial remains of the Western Roman Empire, known as the Holy Roman Empire. The Greek-speaking Byzantine Empire, which was centered in Constantinople, grew to encompass vast swaths of the land around the eastern Mediterranean that had been previously occupied by agrarian tribes. The Constantinopolitan Christians and the Roman Christians, with their individual languages and conflicting theologies, were in a constant state of disagreement.

In secularly decentralized Europe and in the Byzantine Empire, wealth was determined by the extent of landholding. In both regions, there arose a class of nobility whose strength depended on fealty to deliver agricultural produce obtained from tenant farmers and peasant manpower as determined by an overlord. The pyramid of power had the king or emperor at the apex. They were above prominent princes, below whom were major nobles who stood above minor nobles. All members of the aristocracy had various levels of peasants who delivered rents in the form of food and labor. In this system, everyone owed an obligation to their superior: peasants to nobles, nobles to princes, princes to kings, and kings to emperors.

The obligation of manpower in the upper reaches of the pyramid was served in the form of fighting men. Peasant archers and foot soldiers were led by mounted nobles or knights. These men could be pressed into service when an overlord wished to crush a weaker neighboring noble.

The warring of nobles was kept in check by their obligations to their superiors, namely kings and emperors. Eventually, a religious form of feudal organization evolved, in which the pope, archbishops, bishops, and monastic abbots all joined the pyramid of power. At the top of this branch was the pope himself, who served as a central authority figure. He was often much stronger than his lay competitors. In a world of obligations where allegiances were formed and broken, Europe tended to be more fractured than unified.

The friction between the Church in Europe and the secular nobles, kings, and Holy Roman emperors was virtually continuous from the deposition of the last Roman emperor, which signaled the beginning of the Middle Ages, also known as the Dark Ages. The pope would often claim what secular leaders considered to be their domain, and this led to constant declared and undeclared wars. Although it did not end the conflict between secular and ecclesiastical leaders, the idea of unifying Europe in a great Crusade to liberate the Holy Land from non-Christian control contributed to an unprecedented era of on-and-off cooperation among secular leaders. It was also the first time since the fall of the Roman Empire that Europeans made a concerted military and commercial foray into the East.

Ever since Roman Emperor Constantine converted to Christianity in around 312 CE, faithful adherents were encouraged to visit the sites in the Holy Land where Christ, incarnated as a human, had walked the earth. For several centuries, pilgrims were generally unimpeded in their travels to Bethlehem, Jerusalem, and nearby towns. The major danger on their travels from one site to another was local bandits. This changed dramatically with the rise of a competing monotheistic religion that was based on the teachings of the prophet Muhammad (c. 570 CE–632 CE).

During the period when the peoples of Europe were reshaping territories that were once the provinces of the Roman Empire, quite a different evolution of social organization occurred in China. Because the people of China were, for the most part, sedentary agriculturalists, the first form of centralized, imperial governance was created in the Han dynasty (206 BCE– 220 CE). This system of governance persisted through the several dynasties that succeeded the Han, and it survived after the conquest of China, which was conquered by the Mongols in the early 13th century CE. Indeed, the Chinese imperial bureaucracy based on a refined meritocracy among officials was so strong that it thrived until the collapse of dynastic China in the early 20th century.

When the Chinese and later the Mongols wished to expand their trade beyond existing frontiers to acquire prized goods from their neighbors, they accomplished this by military conquest. After subjugating tribal authority, the Chinese enforced their control through the imposition of a sophisticated administration. Order was established so that agreements between parties regarding commercial transactions could be enforced. When trade was interrupted by the incursions of hostile raiders, Chinese administrators raised armies to ensure the safety of traveling merchants.

As a result of Chinese expansionism, some of the cultures of Central Asia were permanently annexed into the Chinese Empire. Under the Chinese system of administration, these cultures gradually transformed from nomadic herders to living in settled urban communities. These communities frequently become highly developed transit points for trade all along the east-west and north-south routes of the Silk Road to Pakistan, Afghanistan, and India.

The Chinese system of governance, which created a fruitful environment for cultural advancement, also promoted economic growth. For example, in the Song dynasty (960–1279), banknotes were introduced for trading purposes for the first time, gunpowder was first used in battle, and the civil service was expanded. The scholars/administrators, who were selected by competitive examinations, proved to be qualified in serving the state and promoting commercial expansion. Meritocracy and social mobility were further enhanced by the rising ubiquity of printing, which allowed for the growth of a widespread educated class. What was peculiar was the generally peaceful coexistence of religious-philosophical traditions within China. Buddhism and Daoism were both polytheistic and were more concerned with promoting an ideal way of living, as did the philosophy of Confucianism. From time to time, religions contended for importance in the imperial Chinese court, but the few outbreaks of violence were short-lived.

In the West, the conflict between two monotheistic faiths, Islam and Christianity, moved Christian Europeans to focus attention on the Near East. By being in this region, they could more easily make trading forays eastward, although these expeditions were disrupted when warfare broke out. The incredibly swift spread of Islam after the death of the prophet Muhammad in 632 CE served to motivate Christians in the West to counter what they considered to be a heretical faith. Jerusalem, which was then under the authority of the Byzantine Empire, was besieged by Muslim forces and fell to Caliph Umar in 637 CE. Christians living in the Holy Land were afforded tolerance; some, such as John of Damascus, even held office in the calif's court. This peaceful coexistence ended when a rival Muslim dynasty, the Fatimid Caliphate (909–1171), centered in Cairo, won control of the Holy Land. The violence against Christians in Palestine and Syria, which was a policy of the sixth Fatimid caliph, Al-Hakim bi-Amr Allah (996–1021), reached a peak when the Holy Sepulchre was destroyed. This spurred the Church in Europe to launch a Crusade to protect Christian pilgrims and maintain the integrity of holy sites.

When Persia was conquered by the Muslims in the 7th century, the sway of Islam was extended into the Caucasus, the region between the Black and Caspian Seas, by missionaries. Islam also spread quickly into Central Asia through Umayyad missionaries in the 8th century. Since the territories separating Europe from the Far East had largely converted to Islam, any notions of Europeans traveling overland to China, if they even knew such a place existed, were out of the question. Even if they could overcome hostile tribes and uncompromising Muslims, what riches might be obtainable from the Far East were completely unknown. If a European noble wished to expand his wealth, the only means he might consider was to appropriate the lands of an equally ennobled neighbor. Thus, kings vied with kings, and their underlings did likewise. For the most part, Europe was in constant turmoil over suzerainty, that is, who was beholden to whom and who owed allegiance to whom. Wealth depended on fighting skills, intermarriage, and advantageous treaties. The latter two created peace, which meant that the challenge of knightly warfare was removed. In such circumstances, the sport of combat was perpetuated by ritual tournaments, which sharpened combatants' skills.

It was in the First Crusade, initiated by Pope Urban II in 1095, that European princes, knights, and nobles hoped to successfully exercise their superior fighting skills with Muslim warriors. Most were completely in the dark as to how difficult the overland and sea routes were to the Holy Land, and almost all of the European fighters had no clear picture of the foes they were to face in the East. The noble knights were encouraged to take up the cross or join the Crusade by monastic preachers, who were sent out as emissaries of the pope. It has been suggested that the pope was initially inspired to respond to the emperor of Byzantium's plea to rid his territories in Asia Minor of the Muslim Turks because he thought it would be a good chance to unify the Christian Church under his authority. In 1054, the Greek Church in the East and the Latin Church in the West parted ways in what became known as the Great Schism. It is surmised that Urban II was dissuaded from raising an army to unify the Church and settled on the more popular call for Christian soldiers to take up the cross and go to the Holy Land to relieve Christian pilgrims from their harassment by the Muslims. But it was not only the protection of Christian pilgrims in the Holy Land that motivated European fighters and their overlords to risk a dangerous journey either overland or by sea to the East. There was always the possibility of acquiring booty and perhaps even expanding a noble's suzerainty over greater swaths of land, this case in the Holy Land. So, a Crusader was not just motivated by a pious belief in the superiority of the Christian God over the Muslim God, but he was also given an opportunity to exercise his fighting skills and acquire the spoils of war. The last motive was particularly important for knights; since they lacked seniority, they were unlikely to inherit lands in Europe.

The princes and knights of the First Crusade, when they were not jockeying for power amongst themselves, managed to unite and push the Muslims out of much of the Holy Land and Syria. In the aftermath of the Crusaders' successful siege of Jerusalem in 1099, the Holy Land was divided up as a feudal state, based on the European model with fiefdoms under Crusader princes and nobles, all of whom owed allegiance to the king of Jerusalem. Crusading princes, nobles, and knights, who were used to perpetual warfare in Europe, continued to follow this tradition in the Near East. The constant turmoil for power was exacerbated in Palestine and Syria by a continuous series of Muslim raids from within and beyond the Kingdom of Jerusalem. Eventually exhausted by their efforts to keep the Muslim Turks and Fatimids at bay, the Europeans were pushed out of the region.

After the fall of major Christian outposts, such as Edessa in 1144, the Second Crusade was organized in Europe. Upon reaching the Holy Land, the leaders of this Crusade, German Holy Roman Emperor Conrad III and King Louis VII of France, squabbled and failed to change the status quo. What did result from their failed expedition was a flurry of castle building by the Crusaders in the

Near East. These powerful stone structures, which were built according to European designs, were intended to counteract Muslim raiding parties and stabilize the frontiers of Christian fiefdoms.

The Muslim Fatimid Dynasty in Egypt, which had proved to be unsuccessful in wresting the Holy Land and Syria from Christian domination, was overthrown by Saladin, who declared himself the sultan of Egypt and Syria in 1174. He proved to be an excellent leader, and he roundly defeated the Christians. Saladin took Jerusalem and occupied much of Syria. The loss of the Kingdom of Jerusalem led to the calling of the Third Crusade, in which Holy Roman Emperor Frederick Barbarossa, the heir to the throne of England, Prince Richard (later known as Richard the Lionheart), and King Phillip II of France all took part. While Saladin suffered some defeats, the Crusaders, even though they were under the command of illustrious European kings, failed to take Jerusalem.

The Fourth Crusade was organized to carry on where the so-called "Kings' Crusade" had failed: to end Saladin's control of Jerusalem. The fleet carrying the Crusaders, which was provided by the city-state of Venice, made port in Constantinople. The troops from Europe went ashore. Perhaps just looking for a fight or egged on by their leaders who were in serious debt to the Venetians, they laid siege to the capital of the Christian Byzantine Empire. After sacking the city in 1204, the Crusaders established themselves as a Latin Empire in the East, dividing up much of the remains of the Byzantine Empire into vassal Crusader states. These states were held together until the Greek Byzantines reconquered their empire in 1261. During the period of the Latin Empire, the maritime trade of both Genoa and Venice began to expand, taking over what were once Byzantine trade monopolies around the eastern Mediterranean and into the Black Sea. The entrepots on these shores were termini of trade with Persia and beyond.

The idea that fighting in the East was necessary to relieve the Muslim pressure on the Holy Land continued to motivate the nobles and the Church officials of Europe. The Fifth Crusade, which was led by the king of Hungary and the duke of Austria, was launched in 1217. The Crusaders attacked the forces of the Ayyubid sultan of Egypt and laid siege to the city of Damietta, at the mouth of the Nile. Although the siege was successful, the Crusaders squabbled among themselves after a poorly planned push up the Nile. After negotiating a peace treaty, the European adventurers departed and went home.

The Sixth Crusade in 1228 was more successful. Led by Holy Roman Emperor Frederick II, the Crusaders managed to negotiate the return of several cities in the Holy Land to Christian control without engaging in battle; it is possible they amassed solely to demonstrate their power. The Crusaders took over the nominal control of Jerusalem. This peaceful solution to confrontation with the Muslims in the Holy Land ended abruptly in 1244. An army of Khwarezmian fighters appeared on the scene. They had been pushed out of their empire in Central Asia by an invasion of Mongols from the Far East. The Kwarezmians took Jerusalem, massacred the Christians, and destroyed the city's defensive wall.

The arrival of the Mongols in the Near East was the inauguration of substantial relations between the Christian East and the Far East. The Mongols living to the north of the Gobi Desert, who had been under the leadership of Genghis Khan (c. 1162–1227), had abandoned their nomadic lives, unified, and took up the role of fierce warriors in search of the acquisition of booty, agriculture, and other goods in the lands of their neighbors. They first made incursions into China, displacing local bureaucracies, and then their armies swooped across Central Asia, conquering a number of Muslims. Genghis also pushed into Iran, displacing the Kwarezmians. It was while the Kwarezmians were on their way to establishing an alliance with their co-religionists, the Egyptians, that they occupied Jerusalem.

One of the successors to Genghis Khan was the powerful Kublai Khan (r. 1260–1294), Genghis's grandson. Kublai forced the expansion of the Mongol Empire to the west, taking all of Central Asia and much of Eastern Europe. By the time of his death, Kublai's empire included parts of Turkey, Russia, Armenia, Bulgaria, and Georgia. Kiev (Kyiv) was conquered, and Mongol warriors moved into Poland, Hungary, and Dalmatia. With the Mongols well beyond the doorstep of Europe, the pope declared a new Crusade against them. However, he soon changed course. Perhaps realizing the immense power of the Mongol armies, he decided to reinstate the Muslims as the primary enemy of the Church and of the Seventh Crusade. To pursue the papal goal of clearing the Holy Land of Muslims, King Louis IX of France, a devout Christian leader, led an expeditionary force to Egypt. Unfortunately, the king was captured, and a large ransom was demanded for his release.

The Muslim forces in Egypt then moved north into the Holy Land, where they hoped to put a stop to Mongol expansion. The Egyptian general Baibars was successful in his battle in 1260 against the Mongols, who had already sacked Baghdad and captured Aleppo and Damascus. Baibars succeeded in taking most of the Holy Land and Syria.

The notion that European knights could somehow inflict a fatal blow on the Muslims led King Louis IX of France, along with the heir to the English throne, Prince Edward, to attempt an attack on Carthage in Tunisia. The idea was to break the supply line between Egypt and the Muslim Caliphate that controlled much of southern Spain. The attack failed. Louis died, and Prince Edward of England set sail with a small contingent of knights to Acre, the last remaining Christian outpost in the Holy Land. Edward, failing to receive a promise of reinforcements from Europe, which were necessary for his continued war, left Acre and returned home. The city finally fell to the Muslims in 1291.

The relationship between the Mongols and the Christian West was complex. Both were enemies of the Muslims. On the one hand, the Mongols could be allies in fighting the Muslims, but on the other hand, they were aggressively chipping away at Christian Eastern Europe north of the Black Sea. The Christians believed the Mongols were anti-Muslim like them. However, this was not the case, as the Mongols, for the most part, tolerated all religions. Their incursions into Muslim lands were based entirely on their desire to extend their power and increase their wealth. For the Mongols, the expansion of their empire had nothing to do with religion. They had perhaps one thing in common with the crusading knights: their pride in their high-skill level of fighting.

It was known among the Europeans that the Mongols harbored Christians in their empire. These were Nestorians, who were believers in Christ but held different ideas from the Latin Catholics about Christ's incarnation as a human. The ancestors of the Nestorians had settled in Persia in the 5th century CE. A fraudulent letter from the imaginary King Prester John, who claimed to preside over a rich Christian kingdom of Nestorians somewhere in the East, was widely circulated in the West in the 13th century. Christian friars, seeking to join the Nestorians and convert them to the orthodox Catholic religion, traveled from Europe to the court of the Great Khan. Perhaps the most famous account was the story of Marco Polo's travels. This book, which recounted the marvels of the East, was greatly circulated throughout Europe. It relates the tale of a Venetian merchant, Marco Polo, around 1300. Polo, along with his father, uncle, and two Dominican friars representing the pope, traveled from Acre, a port in modern-day Israel. They rode overland through Persia and headed north to what we call today the Silk Road. The expedition arrived in the court of Kublai Khan in his capital of Karakorum in 1275. The Polos remained in the East for seventeen years. During this time, they witnessed the building of Kublai Khan's palace in Beijing, a city that had been recently captured from the Chinese by Kublai's powerful army.

The reports of what Polo saw on his journey and what he experienced was exotic, and it intrigued European adventurers, primarily traders in the city of Venice. Venetian traders were notorious for their ability to acquire the luxuries European aristocrats sought. According to Marco Polo's account of his travels, Kublai Khan's empire, which would eventually include all of China, was full of wondrous goods unknown to Europeans. Like all exotic imperial palaces, that of the magnificent Kublai Khan was dripping with gold and the finest of expensive fabrics. Around the time when Polo's account was circulating the continent, the Great Khan sent an emissary to the West through his subject khanate in Persia. The ambassador met with the pope and proffered an invitation from the Persian khan to send Catholic missionaries to Kublai Khan's court. The pope dispatched two friars and an Italian merchant to proceed to the East and convert the Chinese to the Christian faith. In this case, the pope's ambassadors traveled east through Mongol Persia and then down to India, where they boarded a ship for the remainder of their trip. They arrived in Beijing in 1294. The leader of this mission, Friar John of Montecorvino, initiated a project of converting the Chinese and the occupiers of China, the Mongols, by building two churches in Beijing and translating Psalms and the New Testament into Uyghur, the language of the Mongols. John's mission was so fruitful that after his death, the pope sent fifty missionaries to Beijing. The conversion of the religiously tolerant Mongols came to an abrupt halt when the Chinese overthrew their Mongol overlords in 1368 and established the Ming dynasty. In the early years of this new regime, all Christians were expelled from China.

When the Silk Road was finally under control from one end to the other by the Mongols, it may have seen increasing traffic by

European and Chinese traders. The pacification of predatory tribes along the route and the institution of uniform regulations for travel made trade along the paths through Central Asia a viable proposition. Venetian merchants, who were keen entrepreneurs, were constantly on the lookout for profitable trade opportunities. They took advantage of trade along the Silk Road in the 13th century by buying the goods delivered to various entrepots on the Black Sea and in the Levant. The goods that had made their way to the West from China through Central Asia and Persia were loaded on Venetian vessels and transported to the hungry markets of Europe. The Venetian monopoly on trade with Asia was facilitated by their establishment of a friendly government in Constantinople from 1204 to 1261, as well as their regular service as providers of vessels for Crusaders to sail to the Holy Land.

Reading the history of the Silk Road, along with the history of Europe's Crusades in the Near East, reveals how the East came to discover the West and vice versa. The connection between the two ends of the earth, the East and the West, ceased to be primarily overland or along the Silk Road after the fall of the Mongols. China and the West continued to expand commercial transactions through seaborne trade, which grew in the so-called Age of Discovery, lasting from the 15th to the 17th century.

Part 1: The Crusades

A Captivating Guide to the Military Expeditions During the Middle Ages That Departed from Europe with the Goal to Free Jerusalem and Aid Christianity in the Holy Land

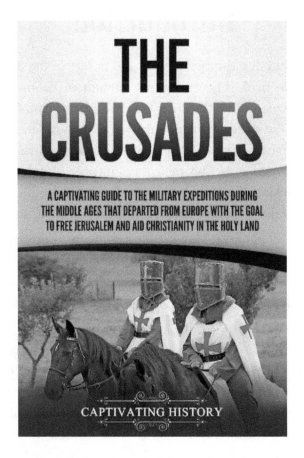

Introduction

It could be said that European kings and nobles in the Middle Ages were Crusade mad. The enormous amount of fighting men who periodically sailed off to the Near East to do battle with Muslims are evidence of the widespread popularity of overseas adventurism at the time. The notion of a Crusade, in which large armies assembled from various regions of Europe for the purpose of doing battle with Turkish and Arab Muslims, became so fixed that it was expanded to include Crusades against heretical European Christian sects.

There are many reasons why so many European nobles answered the call to take the cross, and they all are to be found in the complex organization of medieval feudal society, which evolved at varying rates among the diverse cultures of Europe.

When, in the Early Middle Ages, the centralized secular order in Western Europe crumbled with the collapse of the Roman Empire, there arose a plethora of quasi-states. These states were established among groups of people who shared common ethnic origins in the tribes of barbarians who had swept across the continent in waves. The absence of firm national or cultural borders meant that the states were constantly jockeying for dominance over lands—the major source of wealth. A culture of warfare arose, and it became ingrained in the organization of all of the disparate cultural groups.

The chaos of multi-ethnic and multi-lingual states in constant struggle with powerful and weak neighbors was balanced by a single unifying force, the Catholic Church. At times, the authority of the Church, led by the pope and organized under a hierarchy of ecclesiastical officials, came under fire. Disputes arose over the power of the Church to appoint secular officials and leaders. Also, in constant contention was the direct authority of the papacy over states producing revenues that the secular lords coveted.

In cases where diplomacy failed, and it did so more often than not, the leaders of states sallied forth from their fortified homes or castles to do battle with their neighbors, whether they be other secular lords or ecclesiastical officials, such as archbishops, bishops, or the pope himself, all of whom had armies at their disposal. As wealth was determined by territorial power, warfare was virtually constant. It was the determining factor in the organization of society.

Fighting became infused with the notions of honor, loyalty, and courage. Overlaying this were the Christian concepts of a just war, mercy, and morality. Thus, fighting men of the upper class and their retainers, prior to advancing into battle, engaged in Christian ritual prayer, pleading in advance for the forgiveness of any sins they might commit on the battlefield.

Because warfare was conducted for the purpose of acquiring land and expanding manpower for armies, a complex system of land ownership evolved. As it is said, to the victor go the spoils. In the Middle Ages, this did not generally mean the complete destruction of the estates of the defeated nobles. Rather, the defeated leader kept his rent-producing peasant farmers and turned over a portion of this income. The defeated leader and his fighting men were required to swear allegiance through the ritual of paying homage to the victor. The fealty of the defeated meant that the victorious lord could demand military service from an expanded army of knights and lower-class foot soldiers. The might of a lord was directly dependent on the quality and quantity of his own fighting men as well as those who, by means of conquest, served as his vassals.

Warfare was not the only way medieval nobles expanded their power. Through an intricate system of intermarriage among the powerful families, some semblance of order was obtained in which equally strong kings and nobles could, from time to time, let down their guard against avaricious neighbors, freeing them to attack lesser lords. Intermarriage was also important in securing alliances with non-vassal states should the need arise. Finally, intermarriage among the upper classes could support claims of authority by a noble or a king over the lands inherited by their offspring.

The Church was an integral part of this mix of interconnected alliances and vassal states. The papacy, at times, was equivalent to the noble landowners. Its lands or states were formed out of the same arrangement of vassal states from which armies could be raised. Owing an obligation to the pope, a kind of religious homage, were the archbishops, bishops, and abbots of monastic establishments. These officials were landowners in their own right and thus could call on their vassals to field fighting men when the need arose.

With a culture of warfare being prominent among the nobility of medieval Europe, it is easy to understand the attraction of engaging in wars in far-flung lands. When the pope called for the powerful leaders of Christendom to take up arms against the Muslims in the East, known as taking the cross of Christ, he was speaking to receptive ears. Not only were the nobles inclined to see their participation in the Crusades as an honorable way to demonstrate religious fervor, but they also saw them as a means of exercising their skill in fighting and, for the vassals, their loyalty to their overlord. The attraction of participating in the Crusades, perhaps the greatest one among certain kings and nobles, was the potential of acquiring lands, treasure, and fighters in a region that was untapped by the European feudal system.

The primary function of a knight was to fight. Even during intermissions between serious warfare, knights honed their skills and won honor in ritual tournaments. In one sense, the Crusades filled a vacuum for knights, much as the tournaments did. This explains why when a king or a noble was engaged in warfare at home in Europe, he felt no need to answer the pope's call to serve abroad. Ignoring the demands of the Church, even to the point of excommunication, was a reasonable way for a secular leader to exhibit his independence.

In retrospect, it is difficult to imagine why, over and over again, the call to fight in the Crusades resulted in the successful raising of huge forces of fighting men. The promises of adventure and wealth were strong motivators, that is for certain. The almost complete ignorance of the dangers of traveling so far to engage in war against a mysterious foe also explains in part the eagerness of Europeans to leave home and journey by land and sea to the Holy Land. It is certain that the Crusaders were oblivious to the fact that if they went overland to Jerusalem, they would have to face strong opposition on their way. They would have to depend on the locals along the way for supplies of food for the men and their horses and that they would have to overcome disease while making their way through virtually impassable terrain. If the Crusaders journeyed to the Holy Land by sea, they would inevitably be subject to shipwreck and attacks by hostile powers and pirates.

If the kings and knights who took the cross were unaware of what lay before them on their expeditions to the Near East, the vast majority of the Crusaders were even more lacking in knowledge. These were the foot soldiers, servants, and peasant workers who accompanied the wealthy knights. Among the foot soldiers were trained crossbowmen and spear-bearing infantry. They were drafted from amongst the lower classes of the nobles' and their vassals' estates. Similarly, the enormous number of servants, required for all kinds of duties from feeding the horses, tending to the armor and swords, setting up camp, and managing horses and carts carrying supplies, were undoubtedly unaware of the trials and tribulations they would encounter abroad. The death toll among the lower-class Crusaders, particularly the noncombatants, was not recorded, as the chroniclers of the time would have seen their significance to the Crusades as being very minimal.

There were two Crusades that fell outside the usual expeditions of wealthy, aggressive, adventure-seeking knights. The People's Crusade of 1096 and the Children's Crusade of 1212 were organized among the lower classes who were convinced by charismatic leaders to set off to the Holy Land and deal with the Muslims either through force or through conversion to Christianity. The lower-class Crusaders were entirely unequipped to do either, let alone succeed in making the long journey east with limited resources.

Whether they were motivated by the promise of adventure or wealth, many Crusaders when they reached the Holy Land settled into a life that mirrored that which they led at home. On their journeys to the East, in the absence of Muslim opponents, they attacked Jews, Byzantine Christians, and non-supportive kings and nobles. While on marches to the East and when they had settled in the Holy Land, the Crusaders, in lulls between engaging with real or imagined enemies, squabbled and fought amongst themselves. Because they lived to fight, many of the Crusaders behaved abominably toward their fellow Christians. The knights of one noble were likely to turn on those of another in disputes over the division of spoils or their superior's tactics in war. These were men who thrived on fighting, so when the enemy was not in sight, they drew swords with each other over even the most minuscule of differences. The impossibility of controlling the Crusaders is evident in several of the expeditions.

Because the Crusaders were primarily fighters, their equipment and tactics are of great importance to understanding their successes and failures in dealing with their opponents. The arms and armor used by medieval knights during the Crusades evolved throughout that period of time to become increasingly elaborate. In the First Crusade, mounted warriors wore a suit of chainmail from head to foot and carried shields or bucklers and simple broadswords. As time passed, plates of hardened or carburized iron were added to protect vulnerable parts of the body. The most well-known armor, the full plate suit, was not common until well after the end of the Crusades.

The arming sword, or knightly sword, was a single-handed, double-edged, cruciform sword that was utilized for thrusting or cutting in combat. In the late 12th century, the arming sword came in two forms. As armor became increasingly dominated by of the use of plates, a blunt, short, heavy version of the arming sword was used to inflict blunt trauma through armor, and a narrow-pointed version was used to pierce the enemy's armor. Eventually, both types were replaced by the broadsword or longsword that was wielded by one or both hands. A third type of sword, a single-edged sword, similar to a Persian scimitar, might have been the preferred weapon of some knights. These swords were weighted toward the hand so that the blade could be wielded with lightning speed. Knights also carried daggers, which were essentially short double-edged swords that could be carried at the small of the back or girdle.

Foot soldiers carried maces or clubs with a wooden or metal shaft and a head of stone, iron, or steel. Maces with longer shafts were also used by cavalrymen. Because maces were easy to make, they became the favored weapon of the peasant class.

Along with maces and axes, the foot soldiers wielded a spear or a lance that had a wooden shaft with a sharpened head at the end, either made from the wood itself or as a forged metal attachment. By the time of the Crusades, spears were held by soldiers rather than hurled at the enemy. Depending on the country of origin, the Crusaders had specialized weapons. For example, the Danish carried broadaxes, and pikes, which were 3- to 6-meter-long (around 10 to 19.5 feet) thrusting weapons, were used by the infantry of Flanders and Scotland.

During the Crusades, in pitched battles or planned military encounters on a prearranged battleground, the commander would deploy infantrymen to stand against the opposing infantry. Any break in the lines was exploited by a charge of the knights. If they were successful in this charge, the knights would turn their horses and attack the enemy infantry from the rear or attack the enemy's mounted soldiers head-on. In the first stage of a pitched battle, the goal was to incapacitate individuals among the enemy forces and thus compel a retreat. It was in a retreat that Muslim and Crusader armies faced the greatest danger. Foot soldiers and cavalries were particularly vulnerable if they were attacked from behind, and it was thus in a retreat that many were killed outright. In the time of the Crusades, wounding a soldier was an effective way for their elimination from further combat because, for the most part, most of the wounded died.

The Arabs and Turks who fought against the Crusaders employed foot soldiers with spears as their first line as did the Crusaders themselves. Behind them would be mounted warriors dressed in chainmail and carrying swords, shields, and lances. Muslim cavalry depended on swiftness, and their mounted warriors were less encumbered by heavy armor and swords. The Saracen mounted archers were particularly effective against the Crusader forces. The Crusader crossbowmen were likewise effective on the battlefield and in shooting down upon enemies from siege towers or castle walls.

The Welsh and English were especially skilled in the use of the single-piece longbow (some bows later developed a composite design), and they managed to shoot arrows that could penetrate chainmail. French and German longbowmen were somewhat less talented with the awkward weapon. It took years of practice to perfectly handle the longbow, which in the hands of the most adept could shoot about six arrows per minute. This rate of fire was far greater than competing weapons like the crossbow. The advantage of the crossbow was that it had greater penetrating power and did not require the extended years of training.

The history of the Crusades is complicated. Events in Europe impacted the makeup of the Crusader armies, and events in the East affected the makeup of the Muslim forces. For the Christians, leadership and the depth of allegiance of the nobles to one to another were primarily responsible for battles being won or lost. Honor and greed played equal parts in their successes and failures. Behind the entire enterprise, which endured over three centuries, was the Church, which was no different from secular powers in switching allegiances in the interest of exerting authority and increasing the value of its treasury.

Due to the rise of the Christian Church in the era of the decline of the Roman Empire, the faithful had been encouraged to make pilgrimages to the Holy Land to gaze upon the sites which marked the life of Christ and his mother Mary, as well as his disciples and the early Christian saints. By the 12th century, the route recommended to the pilgrims had become established enough for a German ecclesiastic to write *Guide to the Holy Land* (1172). He described for his limited audience of literate Christians what they could expect to see in Jerusalem, such as the column of the scourging of Christ and the grotto in which the cross was found. He wrote about the Christian sites in Bethlehem, Nazareth, and Damascus. The volume of faithful pilgrims who flocked from Europe and cities in the Byzantine Empire was certainly substantial. It was the safety of these pilgrims and the protection of these venerated sites that was the professed motivation for dispatching the armies of the European kings and nobles to fight in the East. However, there were other motives at play. Among these were regional conflicts over territorial expansion, ecclesiastical differences with secular authority, doctrinal conflicts within the Church, and greed and human aggression.

Chapter 1 – The First Crusade (1095–1099) –The Pope Calls the Faithful to Arms

In the last two decades of the 11th century, the Byzantine Empire's capital, Constantinople, was on the verge of collapse. Invasions from abroad and internal warfare threatened the existence of the empire. Emperor Alexios I Komnenos, who was crowned on April 5th, 1081, was immediately challenged by an incursion into the empire by a force of Norman freebooters from Italy under the leadership of Robert Guiscard. Guiscard, who had set out from Normandy around 1047 with a small following of mounted soldiers, had settled in the Byzantine province of Calabria in Italy by means of force. Through incredible military prowess, he gained authority over the entire population of Normans who had settled before him in southern Italy. After conquering most of Byzantine Sicily, Guiscard sailed with his troops across the Adriatic Sea. In 1081, he defeated the Byzantine soldiers in the outpost at Dyrrhachium, located in present-day Albania. The Normans then chased the defeated Byzantine forces into Greece, where they were threatened with complete annihilation.

It was only by seeking assistance from abroad that Alexios was able to save his provinces in the southern Balkans. He relieved the pressure Guiscard was exerting on the Byzantine soldiers by paying Holy Roman Emperor Henry IV 360,000 gold pieces to step up his attacks on the Normans in Italy. The Italo-Normans were allied with Pope Gregory VII, who had made an enemy of the Holy Roman emperor. Henry IV had claimed that it was his right to appoint church officials—archbishops, bishops, and abbots —or invest ecclesiastical offices within his empire. In effect, this meant that he could demand his share of revenues from ecclesiastical estates. Pope Gregory claimed that the right to fill ecclesiastical offices was his alone. In 1076, Henry was excommunicated for his intransigence in what is known as the Investiture Controversy.

Henry decided to invade Italy to settle his differences with the pope. He attacked the pope's Italo-Norman allies in southern Italy and assumed authority over states directly under the authority of the papacy. In Rome, a party of Italians and Germans arose to combat the pope's broad claim of power. In 1080, a synod of monarchist churchmen unseated Gregory and replaced him with Pope Clement III. Two years later, Emperor Henry attacked Rome. After a siege of seven months, the city fell. Pope Gregory, who refused to accept his replacement as pope, fled to Monte Cassino and then later to Salerno along with his court. Clement III was installed on the papal throne in 1084. A year later, Gregory died in exile.

The Normans, who were the pope's allies in Italy, faced a formidable enemy in Emperor Henry IV, who was prepared to take over their estates. Robert Guiscard was thus forced to abandon his expedition against the Byzantines in the Balkans and return to Italy. This ended the crisis faced by the Byzantine emperor.

The followers of Gregory VII regarded Clement as a usurper, or an antipope. After Gregory's death, they elected a line of popes opposed to the Holy Roman emperor. Among them were Pope

Victor III and Urban II, the latter who served from March 1088 to his death in July 1099.

Urban, who was French by birth, spent the early years of his papacy outside Rome. He was kept away by Antipope Clement III, who was under the protection of the Holy Roman emperor. Among Urban's early successes were the arrangement of diplomatic marriages between powerful Italian families and securing the support of England against his rival pope in Rome.

The ascendancy of Urban's papacy began at the Council of Piacenza, a synod of ecclesiastics and laymen, which was held in the first week of March in 1095. This was a large meeting, consisting of 200 bishops, 4,000 other church leaders, and some 30,000 laymen. As well as denouncing the Antipope Clement III, the council considered the request put forth by an embassy from Byzantine Emperor Alexios I Komnenos. He sought help in recovering Byzantine territory that had been lost by the expanding eastern empire of the Seljuk Turks.

The Sunni Muslim Seljuk Turks had risen to power in Persia and spread like lightning across vast swaths of Asia Minor in the 11th century. After adding Armenia and Georgia to their empire, the Seljuks, under their leader Muhammad bin Dawud Chaghri, more commonly known as Alp Arslan, engaged with the Byzantine forces. The invasion came to a head with Alp Arslan's rout of the Byzantines in the Battle of Manzikert in August 1071 in eastern Asia Minor. The Byzantine emperor at the time, Romanos IV Diogenes, was captured. The defeat threw the Byzantine court into disarray. When he was freed, Romanos' opponents deposed, blinded, and exiled him. He died a slow death from an infection brought on by the removal of his eyes. He was succeeded first by Michael VII Doukas, who was forced to abdicate in 1078 by his generals, and then Nikephoros III, who was also forced to abdicate.

With the coronation of Alexios I Komnenos in 1081, a measure of internal order was restored to the Byzantine Empire, but the presence of the Turks in what had once been Byzantine territory was a constant irritant to the Byzantine emperor and his nobility and presented an unending threat to the stability of the empire. Thus, the call for help went out to Pope Urban II.

Although no action was taken on Alexios' request for military aid at the Council of Piacenza, it was critical to the unfolding of events at the subsequent council of ecclesiastics and laymen held in Clermont, France, that same year. At Clermont, Urban II met with a large congregation of French and Italian bishops to deal with reforms within the Church. In the midst of this council, on November 27th, 1095, Urban II preached to a large crowd of peasants, nobility, and clergy assembled in a field outside Clermont. His persuasive arguments for dealing with the enemy of the Byzantines was framed around the responsibility of Christians to rid the Holy Land of infidels.

Five versions of Urban's sermon were written down later. These were influenced by subsequent events, so none of them can be considered to be the exact words of the pope himself. In one version, he is claimed to have said that his flock of Christians should cease fighting among themselves, cease hating one another, and "Enter upon the road to the Holy Sepulchre; wrest that land from the wicked race."

It is reported that his call for liberating the Holy Land from heathens was greeted with chants from his audience. "It is the will of God! It is the will of God!" No doubt Urban expected this enthusiastic outburst because prior to giving his speech, he had traveled widely in southern France to have preliminary talks with ecclesiastical and secular lords about his idea for a Crusade.

One account of Pope Urban's speech says that he promised, "All who die by the way, whether by land or by sea, or in battle against the pagans, shall have immediate remission of sins." This was to be so because the "despised and base race" who worship demons should never conquer "a people which has the faith of omnipotent God...made glorious with the name of Christ."

Pope Urban set out several reasons for calling for a Crusade against the Turks. He said that it was the duty of Christians to protect their brothers in faith in the East. However, there was also an expansionist tinge to his speech. He believed that the reason there was so much infighting in the West was due to the growing peasant population depending on diminishing quantities of productive land. Not only were the peasants suffering, but their landlords were also being stretched thin because their rental income in the form of agricultural produce was diminishing. Urban also understood the situation that the non-inheriting, impoverished sons of nobles were in. He praised their military prowess and offered them a way to distinguish themselves on the battlefield by engaging in the Crusade. He urged them to stop engaging in raids on their neighbors, in which they sought to demonstrate their knightly skills. Rather, the pope urged them to take up arms with their fellow Christians against the infidels in the East. The opportunity to win remission from their sins was an added bonus. The pope promised those who took the cross that upon their death, a smooth and hasty elevation from limbo or purgatory would occur, allowing them to live an eternal life in heaven.

A successful Crusade against the Muslims in the Holy Land would make it possible for all pilgrims to travel to the holiest of Christian sites without being harassed by non-believers. Christian pilgrims to Jerusalem, said Urban, had suffered awful torture and murder at the hands of the Seljuks. Female pilgrims had even been raped. Urban's condemnation of the Muslims was based on secondhand reports and was in all likelihood to have been somewhat of an exaggeration. Urban reported that the most abominable act suffered by Christians at the hands of the Turks was having their navels perforated and their intestines drawn out and then attached to a stake. The hapless victims were forced to walk around until all of their intestines were pulled out and they died. It is unlikely that Urban was citing firsthand accounts of this way of slowly killing Christians. In all probability, he had most likely been told the story by one of his advisors who, in turn, had adapted it from the story of the martyrdom of St. Erasmus in 303 CE. The Christian Erasmus had suffered extreme torture at the hands of the pagan Romans. The details of this were repeated and magnified in texts recounting the final moments in the lives of Christian martyrs. St. Erasmus, said his biographers, was first enclosed in a barrel into which spikes had been inserted. The barrel was then rolled down a hill. Erasmus' injuries were miraculously healed by an angel. The Romans then coated Erasmus with tar and set him alight, but thanks to the intervention of the angel, he survived. At a loss as to how to dispatch the apparently immortal Erasmus, the Romans slit open his belly, pulled out his intestines, and wound them up on a barrel until he finally died. There was great similarity between the story of the worst torture the Christians supposedly endured at the hands of the Turks and the original tale of Erasmus' martyrdom at the hands of the Romans.

From the earliest days of Christianity, pilgrimages to the Holy Land had been encouraged by Church authorities. Since the fall of the Holy Land to the Muslims in the 7th century, though, pilgrims were exposed to difficult conditions. Nevertheless, the faithful flocked to the East in such numbers that a guidebook was written for them around 1172 by an unknown German named Theoderich. The book outlined an itinerary which took in all the Christian holy sites, such as the Grotto of the Annunciation at Nazareth, the Church of the Holy Sepulchre in Jerusalem, and the town of Jaffa where pilgrims could recall the resurrection of Tabitha by the Apostle Peter.

Historians have delved into the possible motives Urban may have had in making his momentous call for a Crusade against the Muslims in the Holy Land. Clearly, the idea had been planted in his head with Alexios' plea for help in ridding his empire of Turks. Some historians suggest that Urban was motivated by a desire to reunify the Eastern and Western Churches under his sole leadership. In 1054, theological differences and disputes over authority had led to what became known as the Great Schism. The splitting of what is today the Roman Catholic Church and the Eastern Orthodox Church was in the West understood as a direct affront to the authority God bestowed on the pope; of course, the East also felt that it was an affront to the authority of their patriarch.

Some historians have interpreted Urban's call for a Christian Crusade as an attempt to dispose of his rival, Antipope Clement III, who was the spiritual leader of a powerful contingent of imperialist nobles loyal to Henry IV. It may have been Urban's hope that before enthusiastic Crusaders set off for the East, they would swarm down into Italy and deal with Clement III, who was installed in Rome, and his major supporter Henry IV. In sum, if all of Christendom's major warriors were to take up the Crusade many of Urban's problems with the secular world would vanish, at least for a while.

The chroniclers who in the following years wrote down versions of Urban's speech were all in agreement that his sermon was incredibly effective. They all likely exaggerated the reaction among the audience, though. This is probably true for the account that when the pope ended his speech, hundreds in the audience sewed cloth badges with the cross on them onto their tunics, thus indicating that they were immediately taking the cross and joining the Crusade.

The well-trained fighters who accepted Urban II's call to fight against the Turks were convinced to take up arms in the name of God by the many itinerant preachers who fanned out over the countryside taking the message to members of regional noble families and other aristocrats. The actions of three hermit monks living in the forest near Laval, southwest of Paris, are typical of the call to arms during the Crusades. Robert of Arbrissel, Vitalis of Mortain (also known as Vitalis of Savigny), and Bernard of Thiron, like many of their clerical colleagues upon the urging of the pope, quit their lives of seclusion and set out on the road to sway the hearts and minds of all who heard their fiery sermons. Urban himself spent nine months spreading the word in large and small towns in France. By means of letters to bishops and abbots, he spread the word to England, Flanders, and the Italian cities of Genoa and Bologna. In some of his letters, he was specific about the goal of the Crusade. It was to expel the infidels from Jerusalem and turn the city into a Christian community.

One of the first men to take up Urban's cause was Peter the Hermit. The story of this priest of Amiens, France, was recorded in a history called the *Alexiad*. It was written in the late 1140s or early 1150s by Alexios I Komnenos' daughter, Anna Komnene. She wrote that Peter had once attempted to make a pilgrimage to the Holy Land, but he was turned away by the Turks, who he claimed had mistreated him. He became a charismatic, revivalist preacher to peasants, paupers, and perhaps a few knights. There is no historical document confirming that Peter the Hermit was present when Urban delivered his sermon at Clermont in 1095, but thereafter, Peter the Hermit added the call for a Crusade to his addresses to his followers. He used his own experience at the hands of the Turks to inflame thousands to take up the cross and follow him to the Holy Land.

Peter's following of peasants grew rapidly. Suffering from years of drought and disease brought on by poor harvests, peasants and paupers who were wards of the Church were drawn to the Crusade as a means of escaping a life lived in poverty or neglect. A number of minor knights were also enlisted to support what became known as the People's Crusade or the Pauper's Crusade.

Contingents of Peter's army of indigents and impoverished knights marched east toward the Rhine. Spurred on by inflammatory rhetoric by emulators of Peter, a group under Rhineland Count Emicho of Leiningen demonstrated their furor against non-Christians in the spring of 1096, by leveling Jewish communities in France and Germany and massacring their inhabitants. When they arrived at Worms, Emicho's army demanded that the resident Jews convert to Catholicism or either be expelled or killed. About 800 members of the Jewish faith were murdered. Emicho and his followers claimed to be exacting revenge against a race and a religion responsible for the death of Christ. This justified their theft of the money of the Jewish population to finance their Crusade. In Mainz in May 1096, Emicho's army killed over a thousand Jewish people. Smaller towns in the region suffered similar attacks. Having completed his rampage against the Jewish population in the Rhineland, Emicho and his troops set out for the East.

When Emicho's adventurers reached Hungary, their supply of money to purchase food was depleted. So, they turned to pillage. The Hungarians fought back with skill and determination, killing most of Emicho's followers. Emicho himself fled to his home in Germany, where he was roundly criticized for failing to fulfill his vow to capture Jerusalem.

Peter's Crusaders finally assembled on April 12th, 1096 at Cologne, where he intended to continue preaching and gather more supporters. Impatient to get to the Holy Land, some undisciplined French peasant Crusaders rushed off to Hungary, then Belgrade, and then finally to Niš in the Byzantine Empire. They were eventually followed by Peter's 40,000 Crusaders, whom he led from Cologne to Hungary. A dispute over spoils arose at the town of Zemun, and the Crusaders rioted and killed 4,000 of its inhabitants. When they arrived at Niš, another dispute arose, and the Crusaders were routed, and a quarter of their number was killed. The remaining members of Peter's army pushed farther into the Byzantine Empire and were eventually escorted to Constantinople.

The emperor Alexios I Komnenos, unable to feed an army of virtually penniless outsiders, quickly arranged for them to be taken across the Bosporus Straits. They were deposited in Asia Minor on August 6th, 1096, with a friendly warning from the emperor to stay away from the fierce Turks in Anatolia.

The peasant Crusaders proceeded to pillage and destroy the weakest Seljuk towns. When they reached Nicomedia, about 100 kilometers (around 62 miles) east of Constantinople, a dispute between the German and Italian Crusaders and French Crusaders broke out, and both sides elected new leaders who took their followers on raids against different Turkish strongholds. The People's Crusade had now ceased being under the sole control of Peter the Hermit. He returned to Constantinople in the hopes of securing aid from the Byzantine emperor. While he was away, the remaining Crusader army, which numbered around 20,000, departed on October 21, 1096, to attack Nicaea. Along the way, they were ambushed by the Turks and were forced back to their camp to join the women, children, and incapacitated who had been left behind. The Turks succeeded in slaughtering most of the Crusaders; only about 3,000 were able to find refuge and be eventually rescued by the Byzantine army. Peter himself waited out the winter of 1096/1097 in Constantinople. When Pope Urban's Crusaders under the leadership of princes, nobles, and knights reached the city, he joined them on the journey east.

While the People's Crusade was precipitously moving east, Pope Urban's army of princes was departing in Europe. The pope, prior to his speech at Clermont, had secured the support of two of the most powerful leaders of southern France, Adhemar of Le Puy and Raymond IV, Count of Toulouse. The French king, Philip I, was ineligible to join the cause as he had been excommunicated by Pope Urban at the Council of Clermont in 1095 for the sin of bigamy. However, he encouraged his brother, Hugh, Count of Vermandois, to enlist a skilled group of knights from lands east of

Paris. They were joined by some of the survivors of Emicho's aborted Crusade. Hugh's army departed from the port of Bari in southern Italy in August 1096, the date set by Urban for the journey east. In Bari, Hugh met the Norman Prince of Taranto, Bohemond I, who was also preparing to head east with a contingent of soldiers.

Impatient to enter the fray against the Turks, Hugh didn't wait for his fellow Crusader. A boastful man and one who turned out to be a failure as a commander, Hugh wrote to the Byzantine emperor announcing his imminent arrival in Constantinople. His letter was recorded by Anna Komnene, "Know, Emperor, that I am the King of Kings, the greatest of all beneath the heavens. It is my will that you should meet me on my arrival and receive me with the pomp and ceremony due to my noble birth." Despite Hugh's bravado, his arrival in the Byzantine Empire was pathetic. Most of his ships sank in a storm off Dyrrhachium, and many of his knights drowned. He managed to swim ashore where he was arrested by the Byzantine commander of the outpost. Brought to Constantinople, Hugh was forced to swear his fealty to Alexios Komnenos.

The Duke of Lower Lorraine, Godfrey of Bouillon, was inspired by Cluniac monks and took the cross. To finance his expedition, he had to sell two of his estates and borrow money against the value of his castle. In his large army of knights, archers, and foot soldiers were his two brothers, Eustace and Baldwin, both without estates to their name. Perhaps in anticipation of settling in the Holy Land and gaining great riches there, Godfrey took along his wife and children. He set out in August on the land route to Constantinople. When he reached Hungary, his army was waylaid by King Coloman, who, after his encounter with the People's Crusade, was wary of foreigners attacking his people. In negotiations with King Coloman, Godfrey agreed to turn over Baldwin, Baldwin's wife, and children as hostages to provide security that a repeat of the chaos did not occur. Godfrey's army behaved admirably and refrained from fighting the Hungarians. The hostages were released, and the

Crusaders were allowed to proceed. When they reached the Sea of Marmara, Godfrey lost control of his army, and they pillaged the area for some days. After restoring order, he led his troops to Constantinople. They arrived there on December 23, 1096. Emperor Alexios demanded Godfrey's homage, which he secured after threatening to attack the Crusader's camp outside the city walls. Alexios hurriedly had Godfrey and his retinue ferried across the Bosporus in order to avoid any possibility that the Crusaders might attack Constantinople rather than head off to the east.

The next army of Crusaders arrived in Constantinople on April 9, 1097. These men were even more unwelcome by Emperor Alexios. They were led by the Norman Bohemond, the son of Robert Guiscard, the archenemy of Byzantium. Bohemond himself had stayed in Greece after his father departed, and he had defeated Alexios' army in two battles. It was only through enlisting the aid of the Seljuk Turks that Alexios was finally able to push the Normans under Bohemond into a retreat in 1083.

However, Bohemond was there at Alexios' door again, having raised a large contingent of Crusaders that sailed from Bari to the coast of Bulgaria and then traveled by land to Constantinople. Once there, Bohemond judiciously swore an oath of fealty to Alexios, who then provided ships to carry Bohemond's troops across the Bosporus where they joined Godfrey's troops.

Among the first of the French nobles to take up Urban's challenge to free the Holy Land was Raymond IV of Toulouse. An extremely devout man, it was his hope to die in Jerusalem. This may have been due to his age as he was 55, which was close to the end of an average lifespan in the Middle Ages. He may also have desired forgiveness for his sins of twice marrying women to whom he was closely related. For these infractions of Church law on consanguinity, he had been excommunicated.

Raymond set out with his army of Crusaders at the end of October 1096. He was accompanied by his wife and child, as well as

Adhemar, bishop of Le Puy. Raymond marched overland to Dyrrhachium. From there, his army moved into Byzantine territory. When they faced shortages of food, they pillaged the farms and towns along their route to Constantinople. In the absence of Raymond, who had gone ahead to negotiate with Alexios, the French Crusaders were defeated by a large contingent of Byzantine soldiers who were charged with maintaining order among the unruly Crusaders. Meanwhile, Raymond cleverly avoided swearing allegiance to Alexios, preferring instead to pledge his support on the condition that Alexios himself would lead the Crusade. When Raymond's army arrived in Constantinople, they were hastily ferried across the Bosporus to avoid any repeat eruptions of violence on Byzantine soil.

Another leader of an army of Crusaders was Robert II, Duke of Normandy, who was the eldest son of William the Conqueror. Although he had illustrious roots, Robert was in dire straits financially when he answered Urban's call. He mortgaged his land to his brother, King William II of England, to pay for his expedition. Among his retinue were knights from England and Scotland as well as Normandy. Included in their number were his cousin, Robert II, Count of Flanders; his brother-in-law, Stephen, Count of Blois; and a priest, Fulcher of Chartres. The latter was to write a chronicle of the First Crusade in which he included a version of Pope Urban's sermon at Clermont.

Robert led his army south from Normandy, crossing the Alps and traveling to Calabria in southern Italy. Not wanting to risk a winter voyage across the Adriatic Sea, Robert camped there for the winter. When the weather improved in the spring of 1097, a tragic accident occurred. The first vessel to leave the port of Brindisi broke in two. Some 400 fighting men drowned. This disaster motivated some of Robert's men to desert. The remaining troops eventually arrived in Dyrrhachium and moved east to Constantinople, arriving there in early May. Robert did as his fellow

Crusaders had done. He swore allegiance to Alexios, and his army was taken across the Bosporus.

Chapter 2 – The Armies of the First Crusade Engage with the Enemy

Modern historians have come up with approximate numbers for the Crusaders who set out from Europe for the Holy Land in the First Crusade. They calculate from the available evidence that there were as many as 130,000 participants. Of these, about 13,000 were knights and 50,000 were trained foot soldiers, which included crossbowmen and spear-bearers. The remaining 67,000 people were the non-fighting peasants, servants, and assorted noncombatant family members of noble households, which included women, children, clergymen, and, of course, a good number of enterprising male and female camp followers. To field a knight in battle required a good number of support staff—armorers; dressers; men to feed, curry, and saddle horses; and cartmen to transport a knight's tent, food, cooking utensils, luggage, and food for several horses. The knight, and his family if they came along, required cooks and servants. The more important knights and members of royal households also brought along the clerks required for carrying out the duties of a small traveling bureaucracy and priests to deliver the sacrament of Holy Communion before the knights went into battle. In the mass of Crusaders were several clerics to advise the knights on political and religious matters. The priests, clerics, and clerks in turn required a number of servants to assist them in their duties and provide them with adequate accommodations and food.

The loss of numbers due to starvation, disease, desertion, and battles with local peoples on the way through Europe left only about 50,000 Crusaders to assemble in 1097 in the vicinity of Nicaea in Asia Minor.

Emperor Alexios, who many expected to lead the Crusade, opted to stay in his palace in Constantinople. He did send a few of his troops to accompany the Crusaders through Anatolia to help them recover Byzantine states that had been captured by the Turks. Some of the European adventurers, believing that the recovered land was up for grabs, laid claim to it instead. Squabbles arose when they were denied ownership. This episode and the failure of Alexios to provide any kind of leadership and his refusal to provide meaningful military help to the Crusaders turned the knights against the Byzantines. They came to regard them as perfidious, avaricious schemers lacking in a deep commitment to the Christian faith.

The Crusaders surrounded the city of Nicaea in May of 1097. They took advantage of the absence of the Seljuk leader, Kilij Arslan I. He had taken a temporary leave of Nicaea, believing that the assembled Crusaders were as harmless as the peasants of the People's Crusade who his troops had recently slaughtered. Upon his return, Arslan led his army out of the city to engage with Raymond IV, Count of Toulouse's army of Crusaders. Arslan, however, was forced to retreat behind the city walls after learning that Raymond's knights were extremely capable and ferocious fighters. They lopped off the heads of Arslan's soldiers and drew up catapults to knock down the walls of Nicaea. The siege was resisted until Emperor Alexios, having made a secret deal with the Turks, arrived with his army, marched into the city, and laid claim to it for his empire. This confirmed the Crusaders' belief that the Byzantines were not to be trusted.

Like all major military expeditions, the Crusaders, because of their vast numbers, faced logistical problems with respect to the supply of food for the knights, foot soldiers, and the enormous train of noncombatants. Foodstuffs and fodder for horses were purchased or pillaged as the army made its way east. The sparsely populated lands of central Anatolia, through which the main body of the Crusaders passed, was not rich in agricultural produce. Most of the farmland in the region was cultivated by subsistence farmers who provided their landlords with meager rents in the form of grains and hay gleaned from their dry, rocky fields, as well as wool and meat from their livestock. The lack of food and fodder forced the main body of the Crusader army to hasten through Anatolia. Their numbers dwindled as this forced march exhausted many, making them susceptible to disease and death by starvation.

Two of the lesser leaders with Crusader armies, Baldwin of Boulogne, the brother of Godfrey of Bouillon, and Tancred, a Norman from southern Italy who had joined his uncle Bohemond's army, were dispatched to the fertile plains of Cilicia in the southeastern corner of Anatolia to discover if there were sufficient food and fodder to support the main body of Crusaders. Baldwin and Tancred each led small contingents of knights numbering between 100 and 300 men. In spite of having only a few fighting men at his disposal, Tancred succeeded in taking from the Turks the town of Tarsus. When Baldwin arrived, he persuaded Tancred to push on farther east while he organized the occupation of Tarsus. An army of about 300 Italo-Normans arrived at the gates of Tarsus. These soldiers were a straggling contingent of Tancred's army. Baldwin refused them entry into Tarsus, and the Turks took advantage of Baldwin's diminished forces and murdered as many of the Crusaders as they could capture. Some of Baldwin's own knights objected to their leader's rejection of a fellow Crusader army. To vent their frustration and anger, they turned on the remaining Turks in Tarsus and massacred them.

When Baldwin left Tarsus and caught up with Tancred, their two bands of knights squared off against each other, as Tancred's men were indignant at Baldwin's treatment of their countrymen. A few knights were killed in the confrontation, and many were injured. Crusaders fighting among themselves was simply a continuation of the European knightly code of conduct in which the preservation of honor coupled with high-strung, often brutish behavior, was the root cause of squabbles and physical violence. As can be seen, many of the Crusader knights were motivated more by the promise of an adventure than a deeper need to serve the interests of their Christian religion. Baldwin and Tancred negotiated peace and went off in different directions. Baldwin, who had formed an alliance with the Christian Armenian minority in the eastern coastal region of Anatolia, was seen by them as a convenient liberator from the Seljuk Turks.

Antioch, the first goal of the Crusaders when they arrived in the Near East, was incredibly well defended by the Turks. It had extensive, formidable walls interrupted by some 400 towers from which archers could shoot down on a besieging army. On October 20, 1097, the Crusaders laid siege to the fortified city. The Crusaders' optimism for a quick victory faded as winter set in with little progress being made in the fighting with the Turks. Supplies ran short, leading to deaths from disease and starvation; many deserted as well. The siege showed signs of failure when the Crusaders were unable to intercept supplies that the Turks brought into the city. Turkish reinforcements arrived. Their two attempts in December 1097 and February 1098 and their own siege of the Crusaders in June 1098 failed to lift the Crusaders' siege. On all three occasions, the Turks were attacked by the Crusaders on the outskirts of Antioch. In a show of superior military skills, the Crusaders decimated the Turkish relief armies.

It was with the assistance of Firouz, a wealthy Armenian Christian convert to Islam, that the Crusaders finally gained access to the city of Antioch in May 1098. Firouz helped the small detachment of Crusaders to scale the tower he controlled before they opened a gate for the main army of Crusaders to pour through. As they stormed into the city, the Christian inhabitants of Antioch simultaneously rose up against their Turkish overlords. What happened next was a massive slaughter of the Turks, allowing the city to come under Christian control. The Crusaders and the Christians of Antioch were fearful that huge numbers of Turkish troops would soon arrive on their doorstep. The premonition of doom was alleviated somewhat when a local priest related that he had had a dream in which Christ had come to him. He was assured by the Son of God that all would be well in five days. The morale of the Crusader knights was also raised when Peter Bartholomew, a pilgrim from Provence, told them that he had been visited by the spirit of Saint Andrew. The good saint had pointed out to Peter Bartholomew the spot in the Church of Saint Peter where the lance that had pierced the side of Christ at the Crucifixion was buried. Some eager knights entered the Church of Saint Peter and dug up the lance. The holy trophy was held high by a cleric, who, along with a subsequent chronicler of the First Crusade, Raymond of Aguilers, led the Christian army out of the city to engage the relief column of the Turks. It was believed that the assistance of this sacred talisman was responsible for the success of the Crusaders in completely destroying the Turkish force.

With the city of Antioch firmly under Christian control, the Prince of Taranto, Bohemond I, unilaterally claimed the city for himself. He was opposed in this by Raymond IV, Count of Toulouse, who reminded him that both had taken an oath of fealty to the Byzantine emperor. This meant that Antioch was rightfully the property of Emperor Alexios. Bohemond denied that he owed anything to the Byzantine emperor because the emperor had sent none of his troops to assist in the taking of Antioch. Raymond eventually conceded that Bohemond's assumption of the title of Prince of Antioch was legal and just. Doubtless, Raymond anticipated his own assumption of ownership over a more important Crusader goal, Jerusalem.

While Antioch was under siege, Baldwin and his small contingent of knights in Anatolia organized an expedition to assist the Armenian Christian ruler of Edessa, Thoros, in dealing with the Seljuk Turks who were marauding towns near the city. Two Armenian leaders, Fer and Nicusus, joined with Baldwin in February 1098 as he set out to the east to take Edessa. After engaging with the Turks in the countryside around Edessa and occupying the city, Baldwin took advantage of a religious dispute among the Christians of Edessa. Thoros was overthrown and murdered in a riot precipitated by nobles who objected to his Greek Orthodox Christian faith. The theological dispute involved differences in opinion on the true nature of Christ. The insurgent nobles were Monophysites, or believers that Christ has a single divine nature. The Greek Orthodox Church, on the other hand, holds that Christ was both divine and human. With a vacuum of leadership in Edessa, the Christian population accepted Baldwin as the ruler of their city and the surrounding region. Baldwin proceeded to consolidate his hold on what was to become the first Crusader state. He used force, diplomacy, and subterfuge whenever the need arose. He cemented his alliance with the Armenians by marrying the daughter of an Armenian noble.

Raymond of Toulouse, who had ceded Antioch to Bohemond, left the city with his army and laid siege to the city of Ma'arrat al-Numan, located in modern-day Syria, on the road south to Damascus in late 1098. Shortly before, Ma'arrat had been subject to attack by a small contingent of Crusaders, and the Crusaders had been beaten off by an inferior number of Turkish soldiers. So, when Raymond's force arrived, the Turks of Ma'arrat were confident of their victory. Because the Crusader army arrived at

Ma'arrat in late November, a protracted siege was out of the question. With the onset of winter, food supplies were expected to diminish, forcing the retreat of the Crusaders back to Antioch.

The Turkish militia in Ma'arrat held their city for two weeks during which the Crusaders built a siege tower. Shooting down the tower archers succeeded in clearing a section of the wall, and Raymond's infantry was able to gain a foothold on the wall on December 11. To avoid a battle which the Crusaders were clearly going to win, the citizens of Ma'arrat negotiated a surrender in which it was agreed that they would be allowed safe conduct out of the city. The Christian soldiers, breaking the agreement and the ideals of their faith, massacred the Muslims. It was even reported that the starving Christian fighters engaged in cannibalism. The chronicler Fulcher of Chartres wrote;

> I shudder to tell that many of our people, harassed by the madness of excessive hunger, cut pieces from the buttocks of the Saracens [Muslims] already dead there, which they cooked, but when it was not yet roasted enough by the fire, they devoured it with savage mouth.

While the Turks were engaged in defending Antioch, Ma'arrat, and other towns in Syria against Christian attacks, the control of Jerusalem had changed hands. In what is now modern-day Palestine, two groups of Muslims had been contending for ascendancy. The Fatimid Caliphate, centered in Egypt, held sway over much of the region prior to the arrival of the Seljuk Turks from Persia. Under the direction of the vizier for the Fatimids, al-Afdal Shahanshah, the Fatimids forced the Seljuks out of Tyre in 1097, and in 1098, they took Jerusalem. A year later, on June 13, 1099, the Crusaders launched their attack on the Egyptian Muslim forces occupying Jerusalem. They succeeded in breaching the outer walls but were stymied by a lack of ladders in their assault on the inner walls. The lack of supplies for a full-scale siege was remedied when a flotilla of supply ships from Genoa arrived in the port of

Jaffa. The resupplied Crusaders constructed the necessary ladders and built siege towers and catapults. Upon receiving intelligence that al-Afdal had left Cairo with a large force and was on his way to relieve the siege of Jerusalem, the Crusaders hastened their attack. Their eventual success was predicted by a priest who had a vision. He was told that God wanted his forces to fast for three days and then walk barefoot around Jerusalem. With this optimistic message taken to heart, the Crusaders pushed their catapults to the walls of Jerusalem from which they rained down arrows on the defenders. Ladders were brought up, and the Christian army flooded into the city on July 15. Soon, the streets were clogged with the rotting bodies of dead Muslims. On July 22, Godfrey of Bouillon assumed the honorific of Defender of the Holy Sepulchre, and Arnulf of Chocques, one of the clerics in his entourage, was appointed as the Latin Patriarch of Jerusalem.

To ensure that Jerusalem would remain under Christian control, Godfrey of Bouillon led 10,200 troops out of the city on August 10. With bare feet, the Crusaders marched south, accompanied by Arnulf of Chocques carrying a relic of the True Cross, the cross upon which Jesus was crucified, which had been recently discovered by Arnulf of Chocques. In Jerusalem, the former leader of the People's Crusade, Peter the Hermit, led the Christians in prayer.

Outside the city of Ashkelon, also known as Ascalon, on the Mediterranean coast of modern-day Israel, the combined Crusader armies of Godfrey of Bouillon, Raymond IV of Toulouse, and Robert II of Normandy launched a surprise attack on al-Afdal's 20,000 troops while they were sleeping. More than half of al-Afdal's army perished. Al-Afdal managed to escape the massacre by boarding a ship and sailing back to Egypt.

The fall of Jerusalem allowed Godfrey of Bouillon to create the Kingdom of Jerusalem of which he became the ruler. At first, the kingdom was a loose federation of towns and cities that had been captured during the Crusade, but at the height of its power in the

12th century, the kingdom included the territory of modern-day Israel, Palestine, and the southern parts of Lebanon. Three other Crusader states were founded around this time, located farther north—the County of Tripoli under Raymond IV of Toulouse, the Principality of Antioch under Bohemond, and the County of Edessa under Baldwin of Boulogne. Godfrey's system for organizing the Kingdom of Jerusalem followed the pattern of feudalism in Europe. He created fiefdoms for his most important followers who were then obliged to supply knights and foot soldiers for the defense of the kingdom. Unlike in Europe, the fiefdoms were not self-sustaining agricultural communities. In the place of revenue from in-kind rents, the fiefdoms in this region were financed directly from the treasury of Jerusalem. From Jerusalem, Godfrey launched attacks in 1100 on Acre, Ascalon, Jaffa, and Caesarea, forcing these cities to become tributaries.

On July 18, 1100, Godfrey died unexpectedly. The circumstances of his death are not clear. According to a contemporary Arab chronicler, Ibn al-Qalanisi, it is said that he was killed by an arrow in a battle at Acre. Two contemporary Christian writers say that he became sick in Caesarea and died. Of course, there were rumors that he was poisoned, but this was standard fare at the time in the accounts of the death of the powerful, who invariably had real and imagined enemies.

Chapter 3 – The Aftermath of the First Crusade

With Edessa firmly under his control, Baldwin of Boulogne and some of his knights set out on a pilgrimage to the Christian city of Jerusalem. Along the way, they suffered casualties in battles with the Muslims. The small band of knights reached their destination on December 21, 1099. After visiting the holy places, Baldwin returned to Edessa. When Godfrey, ruler of the Kingdom of Jerusalem, died in 1100, there was a struggle among his retainers for the throne. The Latin Patriarch of Jerusalem, Arnulf of Chocques, sent a delegation to Edessa, asking that Godfrey's brother, Baldwin, return posthaste to Jerusalem and take on the role as the leader there. He accepted the invitation and set out on October 2, 1100, with about 200 knights and perhaps double that number of foot soldiers. He was welcomed in Jerusalem where he took on the title of prince and was subsequently crowned king on Christmas Day, 1100. He put Edessa under the control of his cousin, Baldwin of Le Bourg.

After the conquest of Jerusalem, many of the Crusaders returned home. The garrison under King Baldwin is estimated to have consisted of as few as 300 knights. Fulcher of Chartres wrote, "We scarcely dared to assemble our knights when we wished to plan some feat against our enemies." Nevertheless, under Baldwin's leadership, the area around Jerusalem was pacified. The arrival of about 5,000 Norwegian Crusaders under King Sigurd I Magnusson in 1100 served to alleviate the crisis caused by the shortage of fighters. The Crusaders solidified their position by capturing the ports of Acre in 1104 and Beirut in 1100 and Sidon in 1111. This permitted the Kingdom of Jerusalem to be supported by maritime trade with Genoa, Pisa, and Venice. The greatest contributions to the treasury, however, were revenues derived from pilgrims, taxes on Arab caravans moving through the kingdom, and subsidies from Europe.

Baldwin was intent on expanding the territory of the Kingdom of Jerusalem. Among the many expeditions against the Turks and the Egyptian Fatimid Muslims was one against Damascus. However, in the Battle of Al-Sannabra, Baldwin was routed by the Seljuk Turks. As was usual at the time, Baldwin solicited the help of his enemy's enemies. He thus formed an alliance with the dissident Turks. In 1115, he joined with a Turkish leader, Toghtekin, to fight off the Seljuks making incursions on the northern borders.

Freed from threats to the north, Baldwin led an expedition in the fall of 1115 across the Jordan River to deal with the Egyptians. He engaged in a program of castle building, constructing them in territories as they fell under his control. From these castles or military outposts, which stretched from the Gulf of Aqaba nearly to the Dead Sea, Baldwin monitored the movement of the Egyptians and secured a steady source of income from caravans engaged in trade between Egypt and the Far East along the Silk Road.

On an expedition into Egyptian territory, where he captured towns in the Nile Delta, Baldwin fell ill. He was transported back to the frontier where he died on April 2, 1118. His successor as King of Jerusalem, chosen by the knights holding fiefdoms in the kingdom, was Baldwin de Bourg, Count of Edessa. King Baldwin II ruled Jerusalem for thirteen years. During much of his reign, he was absent from Jerusalem, tending to the military needs of the Principality of Antioch. Its army was virtually annihilated by the Muslims on June 29, 1119. Baldwin had some successes in dealing with the crises in the north. In 1131, he fell ill at Antioch. He was taken back to Jerusalem where he died on August 21.

During Baldwin II's reign, a process of assimilation occurred in the Holy Land. Fulcher of Chartres reported that the small number of European residents in the Holy Land soon acquired skills speaking Greek and Arabic and looked upon themselves as being more Levantine than European. It seems that the Christian minority were tolerant of the Islamic majority; they, in turn, were quite happy to husband their flocks unmolested by raiders as well as to render taxes to the Christians, which was at a rate less than other Muslims had to pay in territories controlled by the Fatimids and the Turks. The Christians avoided tensions with the Muslims in their kingdom by letting them worship unmolested and making no effort to convert them.

Because the Crusaders were spread thinly throughout the kingdom, the routes traveled by pilgrims were often dangerous. A major massacre of Christians occurred at Easter in 1119. A band of Muslims from Tyre struck at a large band of pilgrims, killing around 300 and taking the others as slaves. This and other acts of violence against pilgrims deeply upset the French knight Hugues de Payns, Count of Champagne. He obtained the blessings of King Baldwin II and the Latin Patriarch of Jerusalem to establish a military monastic order dedicated to the protection of pilgrims. The order took its name from the Temple Mount. On it stood the captured Al-Aqsa Mosque. Entombed in the earth beneath the mosque were, it was believed, the ruins of King Solomon's Temple. Hugues de Payns' new monastic order, which at first consisted of nine knights, adopted the name Poor Fellow-Soldiers of Christ and of the Temple of Solomon. They are more popularly known as the Knights Templar or more simply the Templars.

Before Jerusalem fell to the Crusaders, a Benedictine monk, Gerard Thom, known as Blessed Gerard, had received permission from the Arabs to found a hospice for pilgrims visiting the holy sites. The need for caring of the pilgrims grew, and Gerard built the Hospital of St. John in the 1060s. Even when Jerusalem was under siege by the Crusaders and the Christians were expelled, Gerard and his few followers were permitted to remain in the city to tend to the sick. When the Crusaders under Godfrey occupied Jerusalem, Gerard's good works were recognized. Later, King Baldwin I and his successor Baldwin II granted the charitable group substantial sums of money. As Gerard received more assistance, he was able to expand his operation to include subsidiary hospitals along the pilgrimage routes in Europe as well as in the Near East. Further, as well as tending to sick and indigent pilgrims in the Holy Land and Europe, Gerard and his fellow monks began to provide military escorts for pilgrims from their arrival in the ports of modern-day Palestine, Israel, Syria, and Lebanon to the holy city. This work demanded that Gerard's men adopt a disciplined military function similar to that of the Templars. They received official recognition and independence from all secular authority through a papal bull issued by Pope Paschal II in February of 1113. Known as the Order of St. John, the Knights Hospitallers followed a monastic rule adapted from that of St. Benedict and St. Augustine. With money flowing in from Europe, the Knights Hospitallers acquired castles and established garrisons manned by knights along the major pilgrimage arteries.

The successes of the First Crusade were to stand as the highpoint in Christian expeditions to the Holy Land. The setbacks that followed the establishment of the Kingdom of Jerusalem were to lead to a series of Crusades that were marked by a combination of Christian nobles' infighting and failures of leadership while simultaneously the Muslims began to unify under stronger leadership which resulted in the loss of Christian control over the Levant.

Chapter 4 – The Second Crusade (1147–1149) The Beginnings of the Kingdom of Jerusalem

Amity between the Muslims and the Christians may have existed in Jerusalem and other major cities in the area, but in the countryside, the kingdom was fraught with constant turmoil. Muslim fighters raided from within and without the kingdom.

In the fall of 1144, Joscelin II, Count of Edessa, formed an alliance with the Ortoquid Turks, also spelled as Artquid Turks, a dissident clan whose land was sandwiched between the Sultanate of Rûm in Anatolia and the Mosul Turks in modern-day Iraq. The Ortoquid soldiers and the Christian knights marched out of Edessa to engage with Imad ad-Din Zengi, the Turkic leader of both Mosul and Aleppo. Zengi outmaneuvered the troops from Edessa, defeating them and began to besiege the city once it no longer had an army to defend it. On Christmas Eve, Zengi's men breached the weak defenses of Edessa. His army proceeded to slaughter the inhabitants until Zengi ordered his men to stop the massacres.

Later, the Latin prisoners were executed, but the native Christians were unharmed.

The struggle to keep the Turks and the Fatimids at bay in the Crusader kingdoms began to collapse with the fall of Edessa in 1144. When news of the disaster at Edessa reached Europe, Pope Eugene III called for the Second Crusade. Eugene was the first pope to come from the Cistercian monastic order. The Cistercians were a particularly austere order of monks who followed the monastic rule of St. Benedict in 516 CE. Eugene was elected pontiff on the same day as his predecessor Pope Lucius II succumbed to a wound sustained by a stone thrown at him by an unruly mob egged on by the insurgent Commune of Rome, a government modeled on the old Roman Republic.

The most influential cleric at the time, the Cistercian Bernard of Clairvaux, although objecting to the choice of Eugene, inserted himself into papal affairs to such an extent that he virtually ruled the Church.

Embroiled in a conflict over the extent of papal authority over secular affairs, Eugene was forced to vacate the city of Rome to escape the wrath of the noble class, retreating northward to France. It was there that he proclaimed, in a papal bull in December 1145, his call for the Second Crusade. His decree, *Quantum praedecessores*, was directed at King Louis VII of France. The French king immediately began preparations for an expedition to the Holy Land. In Germany, the self-styled King of the Romans, Conrad III (he was never crowned as Holy Roman emperor, however), and his nephew, Frederick Barbarossa, were likewise persuaded to join the cause after hearing Bernard of Clairvaux preach about the Crusade. Things got off to a rocky start when the assembly of German Crusaders fell victim to the mania of killing by massacring the Jews in Mainz and Würzburg. The leader of the Cistercian Order, Bernard of Clairvaux, hastened to Germany and demanded that the undisciplined Crusaders cease their attacks on the Jewish community.

Bernard succeeded in terminating the chaos among Conrad's German Crusaders. Upon his urging, they set out from home and traveled, more or less peacefully, overland to Constantinople. They arrived there on September 10, 1147. The violence that accompanied the arrival of the first Crusaders from Europe was repeated again. The Byzantine army defeated Conrad's forces in a battle outside the walls of Constantinople. Byzantine Emperor Manuel I Komnenos quickly arranged for the Crusaders to be transported across the Bosporus. If Conrad and his army were expecting to receive assistance from the Byzantine emperor, they were sorely disappointed. Manuel had already headed off war with the Turks occupying Anatolia by negotiating a truce with them. This meant that he and his army could not march east in support of the Crusaders.

While Conrad was preparing for his Crusade, the pope expanded his call for the removal of Muslims from Christian lands, declaring that the Reconquista of the Iberian Peninsula, which was still under control of the Moors, was a legitimate Crusader objective. English knights who had taken the cross in response to Pope Eugene's bull while sailing south to enter the Mediterranean Sea were diverted to the city of Porto in Portugal. There, they were persuaded to ally themselves with King Alfonso I of Portugal in a siege against the Moorish city of Lisbon. The English Crusaders were promised the spoils of conquest and thus had a particularly strong motive for taking part in the Reconquista. The protracted siege of Lisbon lasted from July 1, 1147, until the Islamic Moors surrendered in October of that year. With their newfound wealth from pillaging, some of the English Crusaders settled in Portugal, becoming permanent landholders; some even joined in the liberation of other Portuguese cities with the objective of sating their passion for fighting and obtaining the spoils of victory. The diversion of the Reconquista left only a few of the English Crusaders eager to board ships and sail to the Holy Land.

Not waiting for the arrival of the French Crusaders, Conrad's expeditionary force pushed on into Seljuk Turk territory in Anatolia. His army did not fare as well as those previously commanded by Godfrey of Bouillon, Baldwin of Boulogne, and Raymond IV of Toulouse in the Battle of Dorylaeum in the First Crusade. Much of Conrad's army perished in the second Battle of Dorylaeum on October 25, 1147. The disastrous reduction in the size of Conrad's following of knights continued even after his army was joined by the French Crusaders. They arrived too late to be of much assistance in dealing with the Turks.

The French Crusaders, under the command of Louis VII, had departed from Metz on June 15, 1147. They traveled overland following the route used by Conrad some months earlier. The assembled French Crusader army was ferried across the Bosporus without gaining any support from Emperor Manuel. However, as mentioned above, the combined armies of Conrad and Louis VII were no match for the powerful Turks. After the second Battle of Dorylaeum, Conrad himself retreated to Constantinople while some of his troops in the company of the French sailed to Antioch. After a short stay in the Byzantine capital, where Conrad was singularly unsuccessful in obtaining the aid of Emperor Manuel, the King of the Romans sailed off to join his army in Syria.

The French Crusaders under the leadership of Louis VII reached Antioch with many troops lost in skirmishes with the Turks and even more succumbing to starvation. The combined Crusader forces did not head east to dislodge the Turks from Edessa, which was the intended focus of Pope Eugene's Crusade to begin with. They instead moved south to Damascus, a target preferred by the King of Jerusalem, Baldwin III, and the Knights Templar.

With Baldwin's army backed up by Louis' troops in the vanguard and the remainder of Conrad's army in the rear, the

Crusaders attacked Damascus from the west. Their approach to the city was strongly opposed by the Turkish army who took advantage of the Crusaders' mistake of choosing a heavily forested route to approach. The Crusaders did succeed, although at great cost, in pushing forward, and on July 24, 1148, they drove the Turks back into the city. They renewed their attack, this time from the east. However, bickering broke out among the Christian knights whose varied allegiances made a unified attack impossible. The siege of Damascus was called off primarily because the Crusader lords who had taken up fiefdoms around Damascus refused to cooperate. With the Turks momentarily expecting reinforcements from as far away as Mosul, proceeding with the siege seemed a fruitless task to several knights. The disputes over strategy among factions of the Crusaders led to Baldwin III and his troops marching off in a huff back to Jerusalem. King Louis and Conrad reluctantly followed. Neither had succeeded in winning anything approaching honor in their Crusade, nor had they even attempted to liberate Edessa as the pope had expected. In Jerusalem, the Crusaders continued their squabbling. Conrad departed for Constantinople to again pursue a private alliance with Emperor Manuel, and King Louis VII, determining that there was no profit to be had in remaining in the Holy Land, returned to France with his army in 1149. Conrad also took himself and his troops back to Germany.

The aftermath of the fiasco of the Second Crusade consisted of consolidation of Christian control over the Levant orders—the Templars and the Hospitallers—the Christians constructed some fifty castles and fortifications. These military establishments were necessary as part of the continuing war of attrition, in which neither the Muslims nor the Christians had gained the upper hand in the territories surrounding the major cities.

King Baldwin III of Jerusalem was struggling with his mother, Queen Melisende, who had served as co-ruler with her son—both were crowned in 1143. He first assumed sole power in 1152 but relented in the face of opposition to his unilateral action. He agreed to put the dispute over control of the kingdom before a court. The court ruled that Baldwin would keep his authority over Galilee, and Melisende would rule the richer Judea and Samaria, which included Jerusalem. Baldwin, not content with the decision, attacked the supporters of Melisende in the south and forced Melisende to seek refuge in the Tower of David in Jerusalem. The two eventually reconciled with Melisende taking on the role of principal advisor to Baldwin and regent when he was away from Jerusalem on his frequent campaigns.

Baldwin was faced with Fatimid Muslims to the south and Seljuk Turks in the north. Both were enemies that had not been dealt with decisively by the Second Crusade. In the north, Aleppo and Edessa were firmly in the hands of Nur ad-Din, the son of Imad ad-Din Zengi, who had died in 1146. Nur ad-Din's successes in fighting off the Crusaders, particularly in the Siege of Damascus, inspired him to attack Antioch, which was under the control of its prince, Raymond of Poitiers. Raymond was defeated in battle and killed, leaving Nur ad-Din in control of most of the territory of the Principality of Antioch. With Nur firmly established in the north, Baldwin III, in 1153, launched a campaign against the Fatimid city of Ashkelon, a Mediterranean port to the west of Jerusalem. Baldwin's army besieged Ashkelon from both the land and the sea. His army prevailed after a lengthy siege, and the city came under Christian control. It was assumed into the County of Jaffa, in which some of the wealthiest Crusader seigneuries, or feudal lordships, were held.

Upon Baldwin's death in February 1163, Amalric I, the second son of Melisende, became King of Jerusalem. His first campaign against the Fatimids in Egypt was launched in 1163. It was partially successful against an enemy that was, at the time, embroiled in dynastic squabbles. Amalric extracted large sums of tribute before calling off his knights and foot soldiers from their looting. In 1164,

Amalric again moved against Egypt, and like his earlier expedition, the goal was not to liberate Christian holy sites from the control of the Muslims but rather to enrich his own treasury and the wealth of his knights. No substantial territorial gains were secured, however. In his absence from Jerusalem, Nur ad-Din defeated a large Christian army in the Battle of Harim (August 12, 1164). Amalric rushed north to the aid of the Christians and managed to save Antioch from the Turks.

In his final incursion into Egypt in 1168, Amalric, having to deal simultaneously with the complication of interference by the Byzantines, made a truce with the new sultan of Egypt, Salah ad-Din. Salah ad-Din, or as he was known to the Christians Saladin, was a Sunni Muslim born in Tikrit in modern-day Iraq. He had risen through the ranks in Nur ad-Din's army. He was dispatched to Egypt in 1164 to interfere in a Fatimid power struggle. Staying on there, he succeeded in winning advancement in the Isma'ili Shia Muslim army and government of Egypt. In 1169, in a rare instance of intersect accord, he was appointed vizier. He proceeded to undermine Fatimid authority, and after the death of the last Fatimid leader, he abolished the Caliphate and aligned Egypt with the Abbasid Caliphate centered in Baghdad. In the following years, Saladin's attempts to conquer the Crusaders failed, but he was successful in defeating the Turks in Syria, taking Damascus in 1174, Edessa and Aleppo in 1175, and in 1183, he assumed an expanded title, indicating that he was not only Sultan of Egypt but also of Syria. In effect, he succeeded in surrounding the Christian Kingdom of Jerusalem. He strengthened his position by making a treaty with the by now virtually powerless Byzantines to fight jointly against the Christians in the Holy Land.

In the pitched Battle of Hattin near Tiberius, located in modern-day Israel, on July 4, 1187, Saladin, leading some 20,000 to 40,000 troops, routed the Christians who fielded about 18,000 to 20,000 men led by 1,200 knights. Thousands of Christian soldiers were killed; only about 200 Crusader knights left the battlefield alive. All of the captured Templars and Hospitallers were beheaded. Guy of Lusignan, crowned King of Jerusalem in 1186, was captured and imprisoned. After this massacre, disheartened Crusaders fled from their castles to hide behind the protective walls of Jerusalem. The safety of this haven ended when it, too, fell to Saladin in early October of 1187. Although Saladin freed thousands of the Christians and allowed the purchasing of the freedom of thousands of other Christians, perhaps as many as 15,000 Christians were sold as slaves. Refugees from Saladin's attacks flocked to the only remaining cities under Christian control—Antioch, Tyre, and Tripoli. Tyre became the object of Saladin's next campaign. It was saved by the Christians, thanks to the strategic skills of Conrad of Montferrat, who arrived from Europe just in the nick of time. He organized the defenders, cleverly destroyed Saladin's fleet blockading the port, and sallied forth from the city and routed Saladin's army.

Chapter 5 – The Third Crusade (1189–1192) – The King's Crusade

The fall of Jerusalem to Saladin caused outrage in Europe. The newly elected pope, Gregory VIII, believed that the loss of the Holy Land was God's punishment for the sins of Christians. He issued a bull calling for a Crusade to restore all of the pilgrimage sites under Christian control.

Henry II of England and Philip II of France, as well as a number of French and Flemish counts, agreed to begin preparations for the Third Crusade that became known in history as the "King's Crusade." The pope convinced Conrad III's successor and cohort during the Second Crusade, Frederick Barbarossa, who was actually crowned as the Holy Roman emperor in 1155, to join the campaign. He took up the cross at Mainz on March 27, 1188. The 67-year-old Frederick was in his own right the most powerful secular leader in Europe. His empire stretched from the Baltic to Italy and from Hungary to France. As such, he was able to enlist an enormous number of knights who owed him fealty. Modern historians estimate the size of his army as ranging from 100,000 men, including 20,000 knights, to a lesser number around 14,000 men and about 4,000 knights.

Frederick Barbarossa led his knights, infantry, and their servants overland, down through Hungary and Serbia to Greece and off into Thrace. There, he came up against the troops of Byzantine Emperor Isaac II Angelos. Isaac, acting in concordance with a treaty he had concluded with Saladin, fought the Crusaders to stop their progress to the east. Frederick's large army quickly defeated the Byzantines, and they were granted safe passage through Constantinople in the fall of 1189 and traveled on to Syria. However, Frederick was killed in an accidental drowning that occurred just short of his goal of Antioch. Many of his troops then deserted to make their way home to Germany. The already weakened German troops that chose to carry on succumbed to disease, thinning their forces even more. As a result, when the German army arrived at Acre, it consisted of as few as 5,000 soldiers. Frederick's successor as the leader of the German forces, his son Frederick VI of Swabia, buried his father in Syria and prepared to recommence attacks on the Muslims.

On July 6, 1189, Henry II, King of England, died before the launch of the new Crusade. He, along with Philip II, King of France, had taken the cross in 1188. Henry's son, Richard I, had independently taken the cross in 1187 in his office as Count of Poitou in France. Richard, also known as Richard Coeur de Lion and more commonly known as Richard the Lionheart, launched an unsuccessful insurgency against his father in 1173. Some historians suspect that his mother, Eleanor of Aquitaine, instigated this revolt. Prince Richard left England and entered his own lands in France, where he firmed up his control by making an alliance first with King Louis VII of France and then with his successor Philip II, known as Philip Augustus. The climax of Richard's revolt came when his army faced off against Henry II's knights in a battle in Ballans in the Nouvelle-Aquitaine region on July 4, 1189. Richard emerged as the victor. After the passing of his father two days later, he declared himself King of England, and on September 3, 1189, he was crowned at Westminster Abbey.

With money in the royal treasury, some of which had been collected as a ten percent tithe levied by Henry II for preparation of the new Crusade after Saladin's victory at Hattin in the Holy Land, Richard was able to raise a substantial Crusader army, which included knights recruited from his English fiefs as well as his dependencies in France, which included Normandy, Aquitaine, Gascony, and Brittany. The departure of Richard's force was delayed because he had to set loyal supporters in place to protect his authority in England and manage his French possessions while he was away. Both Philip and Richard were aware of the danger of attacks on their territories during their absence on the Crusade—both being protective of their suzerainty over parts of France—so it was necessary for them to both depart their kingdoms to ensure that there was no imbalance should war break out.

Richard and Philip, allied only for the purposes of taking the cross, took their armies first to Sicily. The citizens of Messina, fearing the presence of a vast number of foreign troops, revolted. They were soon put down by Richard, who attacked Messina and looted and burned the city. Tensions between Philip, Richard, and the ruler of Sicily, King Tancred, reached a boiling point, but the three managed to sign a peace treaty resolving some of their issues. The major bone of contention was the imprisonment of Richard's sister, Joan of England. As was common in medieval diplomacy, she had been married to King William II of Sicily in 1177. When William died in November of 1189, his throne was usurped by his cousin, the current King Tancred. The treaty between Philip, Richard, and Tancred secured Joan's freedom, the restitution of her dowry, and established that Richard's nephew and heir, Arthur of Brittany, would marry one of Tancred's daughters.

Royal and noble betrothals and marriages were the cause of much friction throughout the Middle Ages, and a dispute broke out between Philip and Richard over the latter's engagement to Philip's sister, Alys. She was, according to rumors at the time, once the mistress of Richard's father. The French and English kings, perpetually suspicious of each other's motives, agreed to the termination of Alys' betrothal to Richard. In her place, Berengaria, the daughter of the King of Navarre, was promised to Richard. Her suitability as a wife for Richard was, of course, decided on the basis of diplomacy based on her familial connections. In 1190, she was brought to Richard in Sicily by Richard's mother, Eleanor of Aquitaine. There, Richard's sister Joan and Berengaria became fast friends. They both boarded a ship in Richard's fleet that set out from Sicily headed toward the Holy Land.

The ship carrying Joan and Richard's fiancée, Berengaria of Navarre, ran aground on Cyprus. Ashore, their safety was threatened by the island's governor, Isaac Komnenos, the great nephew of Byzantine Emperor Manuel I Komnenos. To come to the rescue of his kin, Richard turned his fleet toward Cyprus, invading the island and deposing Isaac. Having almost lost his betrothed, Richard hastened to sanctify their union, marrying Berengaria in Limassol, Cyprus, on May 12, 1191.

Before the English and French Crusaders reached the coast of the Holy Land, the King of Jerusalem, Guy of Lusignan, who had been released from captivity by Saladin in 1188, had begun a campaign against Saladin's army to restore parts of his kingdom that had been recently lost to the Muslims. He set his eyes on Acre, then one of Saladin's major garrisons. With the Crusader army virtually wiped out in the Battle of Hattin, Guy could only field a small army of about 8,000 infantry and some 600 knights. His initial surprise attack in 1189 failed. He set up camp outside Acre and awaited the arrival of the Crusader fleets. A contingent of Normans from Sicily pulled into the port of Acre, but they abandoned their mission when they learned of the death of their king, William II, on November 11, 1189. They were replaced by a flotilla of Crusaders from Northern Europe that blockaded the port. Guy's forces successfully repelled an attack by Saladin but not before suffering severe losses.

Saladin, with reinforcements brought in by sea and by land, continued to engage with Guy's army, which was strengthened with the addition of Crusaders who had arrived from Europe. In early 1191, Guy, attempting to take advantage of the partial destruction of the walls of Acre, launched an attack. Sadly, for him, it failed. In February, Saladin succeeded in a landward advance. Breaking through the Crusaders' lines, he was able to relieve the defenders of Acre.

In April of 1191, King Philip II's fleet of chartered Genoese ships arrived in the port of Acre, and his army joined in the siege of Saladin's garrison in the city. King Richard I's troops arrived aboard some 100 ships in June. Being the first to arrive in the Holy Land, King Philip took the lead. He built siege engines and trebuchets, or catapults, and trained them on the walls of Acre. Whenever a breach in the walls was made, Saladin's army attacked the Christian encampment. This distraction allowed the defenders of Acre to repair the walls. The standoff came to an end when the garrison offered to surrender to the Crusaders. A peace treaty was negotiated in which Saladin agreed to exchange prisoners with the Crusaders and make three substantial ransom payments of the imprisoned garrison. At the end of July, Philip set sail and returned to France. His departure from the Holy Land was necessary as a crisis loomed in the succession to the leadership of one of his most important dependencies in France, which he feared would be vulnerable to English attacks.

In August of 1191, Richard I, now the sole commander of the Third Crusade, marched south with as many as 4,000 knights and 14,000 infantrymen. Saladin's army followed him. His archers harassed the Crusaders from the rear, but Richard's soldiers held off, turning back to fight them head-on. The discipline of King Richard's men was even remarked upon by Muslim chroniclers of the Crusades. Following the command of their leader Richard, the Crusaders did not respond to being harried by Saladin's archers. The Muslim archers were, in any case, hampered by their use of the recurved bow. The arrows they shot from a distance either fell short of their mark or if they struck Richard's men, were, for the most part, ineffective in penetrating their armor. In contrast, the Crusader archers used the much more powerful and considerably more accurate crossbows. Their shorter bolts were much more deadly at a greater distance and were capable of penetrating the armor of Saladin's soldiers.

Moving south along the coast of modern-day Palestine, Richard's army camped adjacent to the forest of Arsuf. Saladin drew up his army on the open plain inland from the forested region, his forces numbering around 25,000 soldiers. Most of them were mounted archers and light cavalry with a minority being foot soldiers. Modern historians estimate Richard's army at somewhere in the region of 20,000. They were comprised of English, Norman, French, and other European Crusaders, along with fighting men drawn from the knights of the Kingdom of Jerusalem. The entire force was guarded in the rear by the Knights Hospitallers.

On September 7, 1191, Richard's army left their camp, with the Knights Templar standing in the vanguard. They were followed by contingents of troops organized by their European country of origin and, once again, was followed by the Knights Hospitallers. As they approached the forest of Arsuf, Saladin's warriors, concealed among the trees, poured out and attacked Richard's army. As was their custom, archers and spear throwers cleared a path for the thundering horde of mounted archers and sword fighters. As the anonymous author of the contemporary chronicle, *Itinerarium Regis Ricardi*, put it, "In truth, our people, so few in number, were hemmed in by the multitudes of the Saracens, that they had no means of escape."

The repeated attacks of Saladin's troops did not stop Richard's advance. The rearguard Hospitallers, however, did not hold firm to their orders. Impatient at being harried from behind, they turned around and advanced against Saladin's men. Richard, understanding that the Hospitallers were bound to be destroyed in this attack, turned his whole army around and launched an all-out battle. The Crusaders, all of them impatient to get into the fray, completely routed Saladin's army. Richard halted his advance and after reorganizing his troops led a second charge. His personal ferocity in the battle was recorded in the chronicle *Itinerarium*. "The extraordinary king, cut down the Turks in every direction...wherever he turned, brandishing his sword, he carved a wide path for himself." He cut down the enemy "like a reaper with his sickle." After regrouping his men for a second time, Richard launched a third attack, after which Saladin's troops retreated.

The Battle of Arsuf proved the mettle of the Crusaders. Saladin was not invincible as his reputation would have it seem after all. In the aftermath, Richard's Crusaders took the port of Jaffa. Saladin withdrew his troops from several of his garrisons along the coast of modern-day Palestine, and the one he did retain, Darum, modern-day Deir al-Balah, in the Gaza Strip, was later taken by force by King Richard. With the coastal region secure, the Crusaders were poised to take Jerusalem.

In November 1191, Richard's Crusaders advanced on Saladin's forces in Jerusalem. He requested aid from Conrad of Montferrat, the ruler of Tyre. Conrad had been an off-again, on-again supporter of Richard. One of the reasons for this was his allegiance to Byzantine Emperor Isaac II Angelos. After assisting Isaac II in putting down a revolt, Conrad had arrived in the Holy Land in 1187. He entered Tyre at the moment when its ruler was on the verge of surrendering the city to Saladin, who, buoyed by his victory at Hattin, was on the march north. Conrad took control and fought off two sieges by Saladin. In the negotiations for the surrender of

Tyre, Saladin offered to release Conrad's father, William V of Montferrat, and pay off Conrad. Conrad was not tempted. Problems arose for Conrad when Saladin released King Guy of Jerusalem, who had been captured at Hattin in 1187. Upon his release, Guy and his brother, as well as his wife and co-ruler, Sibylla, went to Tyre and demanded that Conrad hand over control of the city. He refused, saying that Guy had forfeited his kingdom with his capture at Hattin. The matter of who should rule the Kingdom of Jerusalem was, according to Guy, a matter to be decided by European kings on their way to the Holy Land. An internecine struggle over the rightful successor to the throne arose. This provides an excellent example of the complex medieval culture of family alliances and the struggle for power.

The king of Jerusalem, Guy of Lusignan, and Queen Sibylla, along with the newly arrived Crusaders, went to Acre, where they put the city under siege. In the midst of the stalemate at Acre, Sibylla died on July 25, 1190. Conrad of Montferrat in Tyre, who had suffered greatly from the aggression of King Guy and Queen Sibylla, objected to the declaration that the heiress to the throne of Jerusalem was Isabella, a half-sister to Sibylla. She was married to the Crusader Humphrey IV of Toron, who occupied a castle in what is now Lebanon. Conrad, allying himself with some fractious courtiers, managed to have Isabella's marriage annulled, and he married her himself. It was in this way that Conrad claimed that he was the rightful king of Jerusalem.

After the fall of Acre, negotiations led to the confirmation that Guy was the rightful king of Jerusalem and that Conrad was to be his successor. This was overturned when it was decided to have a vote among the nobles on who should be king. The dispute centered on the allegiance of the two contenders for the throne. Guy was a vassal of Richard I, and Conrad was supported by his cousin, Leopold V of Austria, a cousin of King Philip II of France. In April of 1192, the barons elected Conrad as the king due to the support he had. To compensate Guy for his loss, Richard I sold him the lordship of Cyprus. He was motivated to do this to avoid having Guy return to Poitou in France where he would be likely to cause trouble in Richard's French domain.

Conrad of Montferrat, however, did not get the prize of being crowned as king of Jerusalem. While walking the streets of Tyre on April 28, 1192, he was stabbed by two Hashshashin, an order of assassins, and was mortally wounded. There was no shortage of suspects of who might have hired the assassins. Some say that it was King Richard himself, others suspect the first husband of Isabella, Humphrey IV of Toron, and some even suggest that it was Saladin himself.

Baldwin IV, King of Jerusalem from 1174 to 1185, had left a will in which he stated that the most legitimate heir should rule as regent until the succession was settled by the kings of England, France, and the Holy Roman emperor. With the passing of Baldwin IV, who had inherited his throne from his father Amalric I, the Kingdom of Jerusalem passed to the underage Baldwin V, or Baldwin of Montferrat, Baldwin IV's nephew. After a reign of a little more than a year, he died in 1186. He was succeeded by Sibylla, one of two surviving children of Amalric.

Prior to her assumption of the throne, Sibylla had been the subject of intense negotiations for an appropriate spouse so she could produce an heir to the throne. Baldwin IV arranged for her to marry William Longsword of Montferrat, who was a cousin of the French king and the Holy Roman emperor. Less than a year into their marriage, William died. Sibylla managed to produce a son, though, whom she called Baldwin. The widow and the heir presumptive to the Kingdom of Jerusalem were seen as excellent prizes by Philip of Flanders, who demanded that she marry one of his vassals. His plan was rebuffed by the court. Other marital alliances were also proposed. Among them were the Crusader knights Baldwin of Ibelin, Guy of Lusignan, and Hugh III of

Burgundy. Any of these alliances would have the benefit of ensuring European military support for the Kingdom of Jerusalem. Sibylla eventually married Guy with whom she co-ruled, producing for him two daughters.

King Richard I of England did not retake Jerusalem. He approached the Holy City two times but was forced to retreat. After being beaten back a second time by Saladin, Richard consulted with his most powerful nobles. The army council was divided. Most wanted to attack Saladin's base of power in Egypt, but the French knights led by the Duke of Burgundy wanted to attack Jerusalem. An abortive attack was made in the south against the Egyptians. This only further divided the contending nobles as to what to do. Richard, now ill and with a mind to return home, made a truce with Saladin on September 2, 1192. Saladin promised Christian pilgrims free access to Jerusalem and agreed to the leveling of his fortifications at Ashkelon.

Like most of the leaders of Crusader armies, Richard was always mindful of threats to his power at home. His brother, John, and King Philip II of France posed a constant danger to his control over his English and French lands. On October 9, 1192, Richard boarded a ship to take him back to Europe. His journey turned out to be even more perilous than remaining in the Holy Land, though. Due to storms, his vessel sought safety in the harbor of the island of Corfu. This put Richard in danger of being captured by the Byzantine emperor, Isaac II Angelos, who was displeased with Richard's conquest of Cyprus and his turning it over to one of his vassals. Richard escaped Corfu disguised as a Knight Templar, but the ship he was traveling on was wrecked near Aquileia, located at the head of the Adriatic Sea. Forced to travel overland, Richard and his troops were captured near Vienna shortly before Christmas by Leopold V, Duke of Austria. He charged Richard with complicity in the assassination of his brother-in-law, Conrad of Montferrat. When he was participating in the Crusade, Leopold suffered the indignity of having his role in the capture of Acre ignored by Richard. He had assumed command of the troops of the Holy Roman Empire on the death of Frederick Barbarossa and felt that he had equipped himself well in the siege and was thus due the same kind of authority as the kings of France and England. His banner was unceremoniously tossed over the city walls by Richard so that only those of the Kingdoms of Jerusalem, England, and France were flying on the ramparts of Acre.

Leopold's imprisonment of Richard the Lionheart was condemned by Pope Celestine III on the grounds that Crusaders performing God's duty were immune from secular authority. The Duke of Austria was thus excommunicated for his actions. Leopold relieved himself of his prisoner by turning him over to Holy Roman Emperor Henry VI. Henry himself had been, in his mind, betrayed by Richard. Specifically, his complaint involved the Plantagenet's support of the family of one of Henry's rebellious nobles, Henry the Lion of Saxony, and his loss of southern Italy to this one-time ally of Richard. Henry held Richard for ransom, hoping to get enough for him to finance an expedition to southern Italy to recoup lands lost to his empire, demanding an enormous sum for the release of the King of England. In response to this, the pope nearly excommunicated him. However, Richard's mother, Eleanor of Aquitaine, worked diligently to raise the ransom. The English were taxed, and the gold and silver of the churches were confiscated. While she was busy gathering the money, Henry received another offer. Richard's brother John and King Philip of France promised a more substantial sum if Henry would hold Richard until the fall of 1194. Henry rejected this offer and set Richard free on February 4, 1194.

While Richard was captive, his brother John revolted, and Philip of France invaded Richard's Duchy of Normandy. Upon his release, Richard hurried to his Norman lands and began a program of improving defenses. His primary construction was an enormous castle, the Château Gaillard, which began in 1196. Such a structure would normally take medieval masons at least ten years to build, but the costly fortifications were completed within two years. The speed of work on this building was a result of Richard's meticulous supervision of the construction. It is likely that Richard himself was the overall architect of Château Gaillard. It was an innovative structure with three perimeter walls enclosing dry moats. The inner keep and concentric walls were fitted with machicolations, or openings suspended outside the walls from which stones or boiling oil or water could be dropped on enemy troops at the base of the walls. This was one of the first uses of machicolations in Europe. Their appearance at Château Gaillard had been attributed to Richard's intense study of Muslim fort building in the Holy Land.

Richard's war against King Philip was supported by several allied nobles holding grudges against the French king. Richard's skill in negotiating with potential supporters was formidable, both while he was on Crusade and while he was securing his holdings in Normandy. In the latter venture, he was supplied with knights from the armies of Baldwin of Flanders and Renaud, Count of Boulogne. Until his death in 1194, Sancho VI of Navarre assisted by forcing Philip to deploy troops to fight him in the south. Richard won several victories over Philip. As was common at the time, a monarch spent a significant amount of time suppressing revolts among his dependent nobles. In one of these expeditions, Richard attacked Aimar V, Viscount of Limoges, and besieged his castle where it was rumored large caches of gold were stored. One evening, Richard, not wearing his chainmail, wandered at the foot of the castle walls, inspecting the work of his sappers. He was shot by a crossbow from above. The removal of the bolt was botched, and the wound became gangrenous. Richard died on April 6, 1199. He was succeeded by his brother King John, who lost almost all of the English lands in France to Philip II.

Chapter 6 – The Fourth Crusade (1202–1204) – The Latin Empire of Constantinople and the Children's Crusade (1212)

The failure of the Third Crusade to restore Jerusalem, the holiest of all Christian places on earth, to Christian control irked European ecclesiastics. First among them was Pope Innocent III, who had been elected to the highest church office in January 1198. He viewed Saladin's capture of Jerusalem in 1187 as a result of the moral degeneration of Christian princes. Because they were wanting in moral authority, Innocent III considered secular authorities unqualified to make appointments to ecclesiastical offices and entirely unjustified in meddling in Church affairs. Partly to emphasize his authority, Innocent III published a papal bull, *Post Miserabile*, in which he called for a new Crusade shortly after his election. He began by stating that the Muslims believed that they had "weakened and shattered the spears of the French" and that they had "crushed the efforts of the English." According to the pope, the Muslims were basking in their defeat of the Christians, saying that their victory was made possible because the Crusaders "prefer to fight each other in turn than to experience once more our might and power." The pope called for ecclesiastics to call for a renewal of the Crusading spirit, for Christians to renew their religious enthusiasm and pay attention "to how our enemies persecute us." Among the most successful in carrying the pope's message to the people was Fulk of Neuilly, a French cleric who persuaded Count Theobald III, Count of Champagne, to take the cross. Theobald was chosen as the first leader of the new Crusade, but he died in 1201. He was replaced as the primary leader of the Crusade by the Italian Boniface I, Marquess of Montferrat, whose father had been on the Second Crusade and whose brothers were William "Longsword," Count of Jaffa and Ascalon (also known as Ashkelon), and King Conrad of Jerusalem. Boniface, according to his friend and court poet, Raimbaut de Vaqueiras, had already engaged in knightly activities that merited the honor of being told about in lyrical ballads. He had rescued an heiress, Jaopina of Ventimiglia, whose uncle imprisoned her in an attempt to steal her inheritance. He also rode to the rescue of Saldina de Mar, the daughter of a Genoese merchant who had been abducted by Boniface's brother-in-law. Boniface kindly restored her to the arms of her lover. Clearly, Boniface of Montferrat had the qualities necessary for leading a Crusade.

When he called for the launch of the Fourth Crusade, Innocent received significant support in France. He funded the campaign by first levying a tax on the clergy, who were to render up one-fortieth of their income, and then cajoling the English monarch, King John, and King Philip II of France to pledge a similar amount of their income to the cause. King John also decided that this tax would be collected throughout his kingdom. This commitment was to have important repercussions on the extent of his power as king.

The first challenge faced by the leader of the Fourth Crusade was securing transport to Egypt, where it was intended to deal a blow against the predominant Muslim power in the east. An agreement was made with the city of Venice, which was led by the blind Doge Enrico Dandolo, to supply a fleet of ships sufficient enough to carry 4,500 knights and their horses, 9,000 squires, and 20,000 infantry soldiers across the Mediterranean. The convoy was to be protected by fifty fighting galleys. Such a large fleet required a year to prepare. New vessels were constructed in the Venetian shipyards, and crews were trained to man them. For their service, the Venetians were to be paid 94,000 marks.

In June of 1202, the fleet was ready, and the Crusaders were assembled to board. Unfortunately, the army of fighting men, most of them from France and Lombardy in northern Italy, fell far short of the amount that was to be paid to the Venetians. The promised payment to the Venetians, which was to be raised by charging each of the knights to travel on the ship, fell some 43,000 marks short of the goal. The Crusaders' predicament was recorded in a chronicle, *On the Conquest of Constantinople*, which was written by one of the Crusaders, Geoffrey of Villehardouin. "Every man in the army was called upon to pay the cost of his passage. A very considerable number said that they could not pay the full amount...The money collected did not amount of half, much less the whole, of the sum required." Unable to fulfill their contract with the Venetians, the nobles debated whether to borrow money or forfeit their deposits and return home. Several of the knights handed over what they had to the Venetians. "It was a marvel to see the many fine table-services of gold and silver plate borne to the Doge's palace to make up the payment due." The Doge of Venice, Enrico Dandolo, agreed to temporarily forgo the remaining debt, expecting to be paid back from the spoils of the Crusade. He also agreed to provide additional Venetian troops for the expedition.

One Sunday, the Venetians gathered at the Church of San Marco of Venice, and the Doge chose to address the Crusaders.

You are associated with the best and bravest people in the world in the highest enterprise anyone has ever undertaken. Now I am an old man, weak and in need of rest, and my health is failing. All the same I realize that no one can control and direct you like myself, who am your lord. If you will consent to my taking the cross so that I can protect and guide you...I shall go to live or die with you and with the pilgrims.

The Venetians and their leader were eager to join the Crusade because they planned to divert the army to Constantinople and restore Alexios IV Angelos, the son of Emperor Isaac II Angelos, to the Byzantine throne. The condition for support demanded by Dandolo, who became the real leader of the Crusade, was that the fleet make a detour on its journey to Egypt and deal with enemies of Venice. No mention was made of the ultimate goal of putting Alexios IV on the imperial throne in Constantinople.

On October 1, 1202, a fleet of more than 200 ships set sail from Venice for Zara, located on the Dalmatian coast in modern-day Croatia, as not enough money had been raised to send them to Egypt. Zara had rebelled against the Venetian Republic in 1183, making it a target that Dandolo found hard to resist. They began the siege on the city on November 13, and the city fell by November 24, with some of the Crusader leaders refusing to take part in the attack because Zara was a Christian city. This marked the first time the Crusaders attacked a Catholic city. Many of the Crusaders, however, sided with Dandolo, seeing this as a minor setback to the more glorious goal of obtaining Jerusalem. Pope Innocent III condemned any attacks on Christians, and in 1203, he excommunicated the entire Crusader army along with the Venetians, although he would later grant absolution to the army.

After the Siege of Zara, the Crusaders proceeded to sack the city. Squabbles arose over the spoils of the battle which the Venetians claimed as rightfully theirs.

Boniface of Montferrat had left the fleet before it sailed from Venice to visit his cousin, Philip of Swabia, King of Germany, who was married to a Byzantine princess, Irene Angelina. Under Philip's protection was the refugee Alexios IV Angelos, who claimed to be the rightful Byzantine emperor. Boniface of Montferrat and Alexios discussed the diversion of the Venetian fleet to Constantinople. Alexios sent messengers to the Crusaders, making extravagant promises of assistance plus money to pay off their debt to the Venetians. The offer was good enough for the indebted Crusaders. They still held the Byzantines in contempt for their treachery during the three previous Crusades, as well as their massacre of Latin Christians some twenty years before, where as many as sixty thousand people were killed or forced to flee Constantinople. The Crusaders had more than enough motive to fight the Byzantines on behalf of Alexios.

While they were stalled in Zara due to winter storms, the Crusaders were apprised of the negotiations between their leader, Boniface of Montferrat, and the son of the deposed emperor of Byzantium, Alexios IV Angelos. During their meeting in Swabia, Montferrat accepted Prince Alexios' offer to pay the Crusaders a huge sum of silver marks, increase their number by the addition of 10,000 Byzantine soldiers, submit the Eastern Church to the authority of Rome, and supply a permanent contingent of Byzantine soldiers to secure the Holy Land. In return for this generous offer, the Venetians and the Crusaders agreed to overthrow the Byzantine emperor, Alexios III Angelos, and install Alexios. Hearing about this, Pope Innocent III issued an order forbidding any more attacks on Christians unless they were hindering the Crusader cause, but he never outrightly condemned this attack on Constantinople. He might have perhaps felt that the capture of Constantinople would be a way to reunite the Eastern and Western Churches once again.

Finally able to move on, the Venetian fleet, commanded by Doge Enrico Dandolo, arrived in the poorly defended harbor of

Constantinople in late June 1203. They attacked and were repulsed from some of the suburbs of the city, so they planned a greater siege for the city itself. The siege started on July 11, but the real fighting didn't begin until July 17. On that day, the Venetians scaled the walls of Constantinople from the seaward side, and part of the Crusader army assembled for battle outside the walls on the landward side. The Byzantine army marched out of the city but quickly withdrew in the face of the superior Crusader army. Emperor Alexios III deserted the city, and the gates were thrown open, with Alexios IV Angelos being proclaimed emperor.

Alexios IV, finding the treasury of Byzantium depleted and unable to gain the support of his nobles and ecclesiastics who hated the interlopers from the Roman Church, was unable to raise sufficient funds to pay his debt to the Crusaders. His subjects objected to his promise to make the Eastern Church subservient to the Western Church, and they refused to serve in the Crusader army commanded by European nobles. In December 1203, war broke out between the disgruntled Byzantines and the Crusaders. In a palace coup in Constantinople toward the end of January 1204, Alexios was overthrown, and he was later strangled in prison on February 8, 1204, on the orders of the usurper Alexios V Doukas.

The Crusaders were now stranded outside Constantinople without the funds necessary to proceed to their goal in the Near East. The Venetians were angered over the fact that the financial rewards for their efforts on behalf of Alexios IV were not to be forthcoming. Montferrat's nobles and the Venetian merchants met to discuss their next course of action. Naturally, they concluded that even if the Byzantine treasury was depleted, there were sufficient treasures to be had within the city to justify a siege. In an attack on Constantinople on April 12, the Venetian galleys pulled up close enough to the city walls to disembark soldiers across flying bridges. The men proceeded to open the city gates, allowing a throng of mounted knights to enter. The next day, the resistance of the city's citizens evaporated with the departure of Alexios V Doukas and most of the Byzantine upper class. The Crusaders and Venetians proceeded to sack the city. It was, according to Villehardouin, "a city richer than any other since the beginning of time. As for the relics, these were beyond all description." They amassed some 900,000 marks worth of treasure. This was apportioned to knights and soldiers based on their rank. Some Crusaders were able to pay off their debt for the cost of their passage to the Venetians, but others were not.

During the following three days, the Crusaders looted the city and terrorized its remaining inhabitants, who had been abandoned by most of the nobility. The sack of Constantinople included the destruction or theft of many ancient and medieval artworks. Four bronze horses that decorated the Hippodrome were carted off by the Venetians to one of their galleys. These 4th-century BCE monumental sculptures were then shipped to Venice and installed over the porch of the San Marco Basilica, where they still stand today. The fate of the bronze horses was not the same as a huge bronze sculpture of Hercules, which could be dated to the 4th century BCE as well. It was toppled from its pedestal and melted down. The Crusaders, who lacked effective leadership, rampaged throughout the city. They not only destroyed the Library of Constantinople, which may have held around 100,000 manuscripts, but they also smashed and melted down the treasures in churches, monasteries, and convents. The Venetian army was more disciplined, and instead of destroying the treasures they found, they collected them and shipped them home. The gold coins acquired in the sack of the city were sufficient to pay the Crusaders' debt to the Venetians with plenty left over to be divided among all of the European knights.

Only a small handful of knights actually made it to the designated goal of the Holy Land. Pope Innocent III, after hearing the news of the destruction of Constantinople, strongly rebuked the knights but did not offer any punishment. In fact, he accepted the stolen treasures that were sent to him and recognized the new authority in the Byzantine Empire.

Now under the control of the Latins, as the Crusaders were called, Constantinople was put under the authority of a new emperor. The choice of the European invaders was Baldwin, Count of Flanders. Baldwin's brother-in-law Philip had married Baldwin's sister, Queen Isabella I of France. Baldwin, whose sister had died in 1190, had taken the cross after negotiating a treaty with his archenemy, the King of France Philip II Augustus, in 1200. He was noted for his piety and virtue, and his capacities as a leader were far superior to the nominal leader of the Crusade, Boniface of Montferrat. Baldwin was crowned emperor on May 16, 1204.

Baldwin's empire was organized as a European feudal state. Nobles were granted fiefdoms in conquered Byzantine territories. After the coronation of Baldwin, an alliance between the Bulgarians and the emperor was negotiated by Pope Innocent III. This was an effort to secure the frontiers of the Latin Empire of Constantinople. However, peace did not endure for long as the Crusaders made incursions into the territories under the control of the Bulgarian king or tsar, Kaloyan. He responded by breaking his alliance with Baldwin and allied Bulgaria with the Greeks in Thrace. In the spring of 1205, the citizens of Adrianople revolted against their Latin overlords. Baldwin led perhaps as few as 4,000 of his troops and Venetian fighters out of Constantinople and laid siege to the city of Adrianople. Kaloyan, after hearing of the siege, brought his army south from Bulgaria. His force consisted of 54,000 men. On April 14, 1205, Kaloyan drew Baldwin's army into an ambush, killing many knights and taking Baldwin prisoner. Baldwin died in prison around 1205 (it is unknown when he actually died because Kaloyan only claimed that Baldwin had without providing sufficient proof) in the medieval capital of Bulgaria, Veliko Tarnovo. The

Venetians, having fulfilled their contract to defend Baldwin until the year 1205, boarded their vessels and sailed home.

Baldwin was succeeded in 1206 by his younger brother, Henry of Flanders, who had distinguished himself in the siege of Constantinople in 1204. Under his leadership, the Latin Empire of Constantinople expanded its control of Byzantine territories. These were ceded by Henry to important Crusader nobles. One of these was Boniface of Montferrat, who took his knights to the second-largest Byzantine city, Thessalonica, where, in spite of Pope Innocent III's instructions that the Crusaders not wage war against Christians, succeeded in taking the city from its Byzantine defenders. He assumed the title of King of Thessaly. Boniface continued his aggression, bringing most of Greece and Macedonia under his control. He was supported in his hostile actions against Byzantine Christians by Emperor Henry. The most successful opponent to the expansion of the Latin Empire of Constantinople was the Tsar of Bulgaria, Kaloyan. Montferrat's rule as King of Thessaly was cut short after two years when he was killed in battle with the Bulgarians on September 4, 1207.

According to historical records, Henry was a magnanimous emperor, even going so far as to enlist advisors and soldiers from among the Byzantine nobility of Constantinople. It was said that, even though a foreigner, he treated the people of the city as if they were his own. An example of this is his countermanding the orders of the papal legate, a personal representative of the pope, who had been sent to Constantinople with the purpose of imprisoning the Orthodox clergy and closing their churches.

Henry's reign came to an end with his death on June 11, 1216. There is no doubt that he was poisoned, but who murdered him or on whose orders it was carried out remains a matter of debate. Many think his second wife, Maria of Bulgaria, daughter of Bulgarian Tsar Kaloyan, had perpetrated the act.

Henry was succeeded by his brother-in-law, Peter II of Courtenay, who had participated in the Third Crusade and fought against enemies of the Church in France. He left his home in northern France and made his way with an entourage of knights to Rome where Pope Honorius III crowned him emperor of Constantinople on April 9, 1217. On his way to Constantinople to claim his empire, he was captured by the Byzantine ruler of Epirus, Theodore Komnenos Doukas. Peter of Courtenay died after two years of imprisonment.

When news of Peter's death reached France, his son, Robert of Courtenay, was declared emperor of Constantinople. On his way to assume leadership of the capital of the Latin Empire, he engaged in battle with Emperor Theodore Doukas of the Empire of Thessalonica, who had only tenuous control over bits and pieces of the empire in Europe. Robert's knights and foot soldiers were defeated, and his authority in Greece was usurped by Theodore Doukas. Robert also had to relinquish control over Anatolia to the so-called Byzantine Emperor of Nicaea, who was a second claimant to the Byzantine imperial throne, Theodore I Lascaris. In a dispute over his proposed marriage and thus succession to the imperial throne, Robert was driven from Constantinople by Burgundian knights. He fled to Rome to seek the assistance of the pope. On his return journey to Constantinople in 1228, he died.

Baldwin II, then an eleven-year-old, was proclaimed emperor under the regency of John of Brienne. Throughout his reign from 1228 to 1273, Baldwin II was constantly in search of money to support the defense of his empire, which consisted of little more than the city itself. He made the rounds of potential financiers in Europe in 1236 and achieved a measure of success. To raise money, he helped himself to the Crown of Thorns, which had been placed on Jesus' head before he was crucified. This had once belonged to the Byzantines but was later pawned to a Venetian merchant as security for a loan. It was taken from them to bring to

Paris and was given to Louis IX in 1238. He built one of the jewels of Gothic architecture, the elegant Sainte-Chapelle, to house this relic. (After the French Revolution, the Crown of Thorns was deposited in Notre Dame Cathedral. It was one of the treasures of the cathedral saved by firemen in the conflagration of April 15, 2019.)

In spite of enlisting some soldiers and raising some badly needed funds, Baldwin was unable to defend Constantinople, and it was overrun by the Greeks on July 24, 1261, thus effectively ending the Latin Empire of Constantinople, although the title was still held until 1383. The Byzantines installed Michael VIII Palaeologus as emperor. Baldwin II escaped and subsequently lived in retirement in France.

Children's Crusade 1212

Because documentary evidence for the Children's Crusade has been considered more stuff of myth and legend than factual, it is not included in the sequential numbering of Christian expeditions to the East. Nevertheless, it is useful to consider this particular Crusade because it sheds light on the ethos of Christian Europe in the midst of the long and enduring passion for the Crusades.

The Children's Crusade, according to what records do exist on it, consisted of two waves. It was said that a German shepherd boy from Cologne, named Nicholas, preached a Crusade to receptive children. These, in turn, persuaded others to join them. Having gathered, a following of disciples, which according to some records may have numbered 21,000, were led across the Alps into Italy by Nicholas. The *Chronica regia Coloniensis,* or *Royal Chronicle of Cologne*, includes the following passage.

> Many thousands of boys, ranging in age from six years to
> full maturity, left the plows or carts they were driving, the
> flocks which they were pasturing, and anything else which
> they were doing. This they did despite the wishes of their
> parents, relatives, and friends who sought to make them

draw back. Suddenly one ran after another to take the cross. Thus, by groups of twenty, or fifty, or a hundred, they put up banners and began to journey to Jerusalem. The children claimed that it was the will of the Divine that prompted them to undertake this Crusade. In spite of this, their expedition did not achieve its intention in the end.

On the journey south, particularly on the treacherous paths through the Alps, two-thirds of the Crusaders died. Their goal was Genoa where, said Nicholas, God would cause the sea to part and the Crusaders could then walk to the Holy Land. When this didn't happen, some turned on Nicholas, and some settled down to await the miraculous appearance of a dry passage to the East. The Genoese, sympathetic to the stranded young Crusaders who were camped on their doorstep, offered them safe haven and absorbed their numbers into the urban population. Nicholas, undeterred by the failure of God to provide a dry path to the Holy Land, led a few of his remaining flock to Rome where they met with Pope Innocent III, who told them that they were too young to go to the East. Nicholas then disappears from historical records. He apparently perished on re-crossing the Alps.

A second wave of youth Crusaders formed in France around the charismatic twelve-year-old Stephen of Cloyes. He said that in a dream he had been given a letter from Christ addressed to the king of France. Stephen gathered 30,000 disciples; this number included some adults who were taken with the piety of the group and impressed by the mystical communion many of the children claimed to have with God. The Crusaders went to Saint-Denis to meet with the French king, Philip II. He was unimpressed by their cause and presumably told them to return to their homes. Undaunted, Stephen went to a nearby abbey and continued to preach his Crusade. As his throng journeyed south, their numbers depleted so that by the time they reached Marseille, perhaps half remained. Unable to find transport to the Holy Land, they disbanded, and those that did not return home were captured by unscrupulous merchants and sold into slavery.

In modern times, several historians have attempted to elicit the meaning of the story of the Children's Crusade. One has said that it represents "diseased religious emotionalism." Another source considers it to be an archetypical moral tale of innocents sacrificing themselves for their faith. Yet another has thought it to be a story of chivalric piety with an anti-war motif. It may, some have written, been a paean of the poor and the dispossessed seeking relief from their misery. A close reading of the texts about the Children's Crusade suggests that the participants were not all children but simply those who suffered under the drudgery of agricultural labor as the *Chronica regia Coloniensis*, written in 1213, suggests in the passage quoted above.

Chapter 7 – The Fifth Crusade (1217–1221)

The diversion of the Fourth Crusade to Constantinople was understood by many in the West as an example of Venetian treachery motivated by the greed of merchants to monopolize maritime trade in the East. Pope Innocent III was disappointed in the Fourth Crusade because it involved only battles with fellow Christians. The Crusaders had done nothing with respect to the removal of Muslims from the Holy Land.

Pope Innocent III had more than Muslim enemies on his mind after the end of the Fourth Crusade. In southern France, a heretical sect of Christians, the Cathars, also known as Albigensians after the town of Albi where the movement first took hold, had usurped the power of the Catholic Church. The Cathars, who believed in two deities, one good and the other evil, declared themselves independent of the authority of the Church, believing it to be thoroughly corrupt and doctrinally in error. The Cathars were, as well, proto-feminists. According to their faith, they held that both women and men could administer the holy sacraments. This was abhorrent to the patriarchal Catholic Church. The killing of his legate to the court of Count Raymond VI of Toulouse in 1208 ended Innocent III's peaceful attempt to convince the Cathars of the errors of their beliefs. He excommunicated Count Raymond, who was not a Cathar himself, for being too lenient in his dealings with the heretical sect. In order to destroy the heretics by means of the sword, Innocent called on the French king, Philip II, to launch a Crusade against the heretics in the south of France. Neither Philip nor his son Louis joined in the expedition; however, many northern nobles rode off to Languedoc, having been promised that they could keep any of the lands that they might capture.

The Crusaders, under the command of the papal legate, the Abbot of Cîteaiux, in their first engagement with the Cathars, attacked the town of Béziers on July 22, 1209, where they massacred some 7,000 inhabitants, making little effort to distinguish between Cathars and Catholics. A long series of sieges and massacres followed, in which the so-called Albigensian Crusaders prevailed over the breakaway sect. The Cathars were subsequently hunted down and executed by the Inquisition, which was established in 1233.

The Crusade against the Cathars was not the only Crusade fought on European soil. In the Iberian Peninsula, the notion of a Crusade was invoked to hasten the removal of the Moors from Spanish and Portuguese lands. The ongoing struggle against the Muslims, or Moors, known as the Reconquista, began to turn in favor of the Christians in a Crusade called by Pope Innocent III. The coalition of monarchs and nobles from Spain and France joined Alfonso VIII, King of Castile, in opposing the Almohad Caliphate leaders from the southern half of the Iberian Peninsula. Under Caliph al-Nasir, an army of North African Muslims crossed the Strait of Gibraltar to firm up Muslim control of Al-Andalus (modern Andalusia). The huge Muslim force threatened to push north and dislodge the Christian forces who were firmly in control of about half of Spain. Alfonso VIII's coalition of French and Spanish nobles and monarchs attacked the Muslims. In the Battle of Las Navas de Tolosa, the Christians surprised the Moors and routed them on July 16, 1212. Alfonso then pushed south toward Andalusia, where his army massacred and enslaved an enormous number of Muslims. Perhaps as many as 100,000 Muslims were captured, according to a contemporary chronicle of the campaign. After the Battle of Las Navas de Tolosa, the Spanish and their allies proceeded to slowly push the Moors out of the Iberian Peninsula. The Reconquista, which lasted 781 years, was completed with the surrender of Granada in 1492.

While the Crusade against the Albigensian heretics was unfolding and the Moors were losing ground in Spain, Innocent issued a papal bull in 1213 and another in 1215 calling for all in Christendom to support a new Crusade to rid the Holy Land of the Muslims. With the failure of the secular leadership of the Fourth Crusade to do anything to further this cause, Pope Innocent III intended to place a new Crusader army under the direct leadership of the Church. The Crusade was to commence in 1217.

The mouthpiece for the pope in France, Cardinal Robert of Courçon, was unsuccessful in convincing French nobles to take the cross. Many of the nobles were fully occupied with forcibly taking the lands of Languedoc in the south from the nobles sympathetic to the Albigensian cause. When Pope Innocent III died suddenly in July 1216, his successor, Pope Honorius III, took up managing the preparations for the Crusade. He committed money from the papal treasury for the massive undertaking and levied a tax on Church officials and all ecclesiastics to pay for the expedition to the Levant. Honorius identified the prime source for Crusaders as the Holy Roman Empire. In spite of continual pressure from the pope, the King of Germany, Frederick II, put off assembling an army and embarking for the Holy Land. He did send some contingents, but these were not of the size he promised.

The only nobles to meet the deadline for the departure of the Crusade were Duke Leopold VI of Austria, Duke Otto I of

Merania, and King Andrew II of Hungary. Their armies converged at Spalato (Split) in Dalmatia and boarded Venetian vessels for transport to Acre. The number of fighting men, perhaps as many as 10,000 knights, was such that they had to be ferried in waves down the Adriatic and eastward across the Mediterranean. The plan to sail on from Acre to Egypt was delayed because King Andrew, who was ill, decided to return home to Hungary in January of 1218. This depleted the army of Crusaders to such an extent that it was decided to wait for reinforcements from Europe. When they eventually arrived, the Crusaders sailed to Damietta at the mouth of the Nile.

Encamped across the Nile from Damietta, the Crusaders launched several attacks against the tower of Damietta. They were driven off each time by the defenders under the command of Sultan Al-Kāmil, the fourth ruler of the Ayyubid dynasty in Egypt that had been founded by Saladin. The Crusaders then developed an ingenious solution to breaching the defenses of Damietta that consisted of 3 walls, 28 towers, and a moat. Using a design created by a Church official, Oliver of Paderborn, who also served as a chronicler of the Crusade, the Christian soldiers tied two ships together and erected a castle-like structure with a lofty flying bridge on them. The contraption was maneuvered next to the tower of Damietta. The siege of the tower had failed for nearly two months; however, in a single day, the siege engine captured the tower. Crusader reinforcements arrived at the end of September 1218. With them was the Spaniard Cardinal Pelagius of Albano, who assumed command of the operation.

In February 1219, Sultan Al-Kāmil, fearing the imminent success of the Crusaders in their siege, rode off from Damietta to modern-day Al Manṣūra farther up the Nile. He deserted his troops, who soon followed him, stealing out of the city. The Crusaders dithered and did not push their advantage, choosing to merely surround the city and wait. Sultan Al-Kāmil attempted to sue for peace, offering to turn over Jerusalem and the surrounding territory if the

Crusaders pulled out of Egypt. Cardinal Pelagius refused this offer, doing so again when the Muslims offered to sweeten the deal with a substantial cash payment. Pelagius' intransigence was foolish as the Crusader camp was diminishing on account of some nobles and their entourages departing for home. He also refused to understand that the Muslim forces were on the verge of receiving reinforcements from troops as far away as Syria.

In the midst of the protracted negotiations at Damietta, an Italian monk, Francis of Assisi, the founder of the Franciscan order, arrived at the Crusaders' camp. His journey from the headquarters of his rapidly expanding order was one of several he undertook to preach the gospel. His intention in appearing at Damietta was to convert the Sultan of Egypt or become a martyr in the attempt. In an interim in the back and forth skirmishes between the Christians and Muslims, Francis, along with a fellow brother, made his way into the sultan's camp. According to the earliest biographies of Francis, he was well received but failed to shake either the sultan's or his advisors' belief in the Quran. Francis left the Crusaders' camp and sailed off to Acre and then to Italy.

In April of 1219, the Crusaders' camp was attacked by strengthened Muslim forces. The Crusaders held them off, and Pelagius then decided to reactivate the siege of Damietta. The determined attack failed, and it was followed by a Muslim ambush of Crusaders in which as many as 4,300 Crusaders were killed. At this point, the Egyptians attempted to negotiate another peace treaty. While it was under discussion in the Crusaders' camp, a vulnerability in the walls of Damietta was discovered by chance. The Crusaders swarmed up ladders and took the city without opposition. The siege of Damietta resulted in the deaths of at least 50,000 people due to lack of supplies and disease. Pelagius, a demanding and thoroughly unsympathetic leader, alienated the leaders of his own army, who disliked his style and objected to his tactics. In the spring of 1220, John of Brienne, the King of Jerusalem, left

Damietta for Acre with his troops, and several Crusaders opted to return home to Europe. The depletion of Crusader forces was compensated by the arrival of contingents of Italian troops led by bishops and archbishops who were all inept commanders.

Throughout the rest of the year, the Crusaders settled into life in Damietta while the Egyptians reinforced their fortifications at Al Manṣūra. With the return of King John of Jerusalem and the arrival of German Crusaders, Pelagius commanded the Crusaders to attack Al Manṣūra. His troops marched south along the banks of the Nile, and they were followed by a fleet of some 600 ships and galleys that sailed up the river. In preparation for a siege of the well-fortified city, the Crusaders set up camp. Pelagius, who was completely lacking in tactical abilities, did not blockade Al Manṣūra, and the Muslim forces in the fort were, essentially, reinforced by Muslim forces from Syria who camped in a location that blocked any possibility of retreat by land from the Crusaders. The Egyptians set traps on the Nile and destroyed the Crusader supply ships. When Pelagius finally understood the danger the Crusaders were in, he ordered a retreat to Damietta. It was a complete fiasco. The Muslims destroyed dikes, flooding the only overland route north. Trapped and lacking supplies, the Crusaders were forced to negotiate an armistice on August 28, 1221. Muslim control over Jerusalem was not relinquished, so Innocent's idea of putting a Crusade under the command of men from the Church proved to be a complete disaster.

Chapter 8 – The Sixth Crusade (1228-1229) – The Holy Roman Emperor Frederick II Takes the Cross

The most powerful ruler in Europe in the first half of the 13th century was Frederick II, Emperor of the Holy Roman Empire. The son of Emperor Henry VI, Frederick was elected King of the Germans in 1196 at the age of two and was appointed King of Sicily at the age of three. His mother, Constance, ruled Sicily as regent, and after her death in 1198, Frederick came under the guardianship of Pope Innocent III. Before he reached the age of majority, Frederick's Kingdom of Sicily had dissolved into a number of independent principalities whose barons and adventurers had usurped imperial authority. Frederick had a similar problem in Germany, where, even after he was crowned as king in 1212, he had to share power with a rival king of Germany, Otto IV. After Otto's death in 1218, Frederick struggled to firm up support among the German nobility, and it was not until 1220 that he was crowned Holy Roman emperor by Pope Honorius III. Frederick spent the first part of his reign in Sicily where he consolidated his hold over the state through the promulgation of the Constitutions of Melfi in 1231. These laws ensured the primacy of written law over local traditions and ensured that Frederick held sway as an absolute monarch.

In 1225, Frederick II married Isabella II, the daughter of John of Brienne, King of Jerusalem. Now free from consolidating his power over his lands in Germany and Italy and with a significant matrimonial alliance that gave him some claim to power in the Holy Land, the emperor assembled his army in Brindisi, Italy. Shortly after they had embarked on their vessels in August of 1227, Frederick's troops began to die from an epidemic disease. The flotilla returned to Brindisi, at which point Pope Gregory IX excommunicated him for his failure to carry out his vow to go on Crusade. The pope had other reasons for punishing Frederick, as the emperor had for many years neglected his duty to the Church by forcefully attempting to expropriate papal lands in Italy.

Frederick ignored his excommunication and set off again for Acre in 1228. On the way, he diverted his fleet to Cyprus. He claimed the island as a fiefdom that had owed homage to the Holy Roman emperor since its capture by Richard the Lionheart during the Third Crusade. He demanded that the regent of Cyprus, John Ibelin, who also was called the Old Lord of Beirut, vacate his authority over Cyprus and Beirut.

Having secured his authority over Cyprus, Frederick sailed to Acre. On his arrival, he found the inhabitants of the city, now the nominal capital of the Kingdom of Jerusalem, to be hostile to his presence. The patriarch, the leader of the Eastern Church, and the clergy, knowing that he had been excommunicated, refused to support his Crusade. The nobles were reluctant to follow his orders, fearing that they would be obliged to make their fiefdoms in Syria dependencies of the Holy Roman emperor. They also held it against Frederick that he had demanded John Ibelin to forfeit his suzerainty over Beirut, the capital of modern-day Lebanon.

The forfeiture of local authority, that is paying homage to a king, prince, or other noble, was a serious matter for the Crusaders who had settled in the Near East. They had much more at stake than mere power. They had settled into a life that paralleled a noble's environment in Europe and benefited from the income provided by their appropriated domains abroad. For example, John Ibelin, in rebuilding Beirut after Saladin's conquest of the city, had erected a grandiose family palace in which he could luxuriate in fabulous surroundings. It was described by a visitor in 1212. The central hall had a pavement "made of marble, which imitates water moved by a light breeze. And this is done so subtly that whoever treads on it feels as if he were wading, marvelling at not leaving any impression of the depicted sand." They had "a fountain with a dragon as the centre-piece stood in the central hall, its jets cooling the air and the murmur of the water giving an altogether soothing effect." The ceiling was painted with a fresco representing the heavens, "with such life-like colours that clouds pass across, the west wind blows, and there the sun seems to mark out the year and the months, the days and the weeks, the hours and the moments by its movement in the zodiac." It is little wonder, having established himself and his court in such magnificent surroundings, that John Ibelin would have feared Frederick's designs on annexing the Holy Land into the Holy Roman Empire. If he were forced to pay homage to Frederick, he would be required to turn over a portion of his income to his superior.

Frederick's army, which was too small to engage with the forces of Sultan Al-Kāmil of Egypt, could only hope for success on his mission by means of negotiation. Fortunately, the sultan was preoccupied with the suppression of rebels in Syria, so he consented to Frederick's terms in a treaty signed on February 18, 1229. In the treaty, he agreed to cede Jerusalem to the Christians along with the important pilgrimage cities of Nazareth and Bethlehem and the cities of Sidon and Jaffa. The Muslims did not turn over control of the Temple Mount, al-Aqsa Mosque, and the Dome of the Rock in Jerusalem. The truce enacted by the treaty was to last ten years.

Frederick, basking in the glory of his diplomatic coup, made a triumphal entry into Jerusalem on March 17, 1229. He proceeded to have himself crowned as King of Jerusalem. In fact, he obtained authority only as regent acting in place of his son, Conrad, who was the heir to the throne of Jerusalem through his mother Isabella II. The Latin Patriarch of Jerusalem, Gerold of Lausanne, who adamantly refused to bow to Frederick's authority, did not preside over the so-called coronation. On the next day, the Latin Patriarch placed the city under an interdict, which is a ban that prohibits people from participating in certain rites.

In May 1229, Frederick left Jerusalem and sailed back to Europe. Although his Crusade involved no battles, he had proved to the European monarchs who were to follow in his footsteps that adventuring in the Holy Land did not require papal authority. His was a purely secular mission.

The nobles and clergy of the Kingdom of Jerusalem refused to accept the departed Frederick's assumption of the kingdom into his empire. The barons, among whom was John Ibelin, who was still smarting over his treatment in Cyprus, was one of those who resisted the representatives of the now-departed Holy Roman emperor. Frederick's viceroy was forced out of Acre within months.

After returning to Europe, Frederick had his excommunication lifted in the Treaty of Ceprano, which was signed in August of 1230. More important was the agreement between Frederick II and Pope Gregory IX to cease hostilities over territories claimed by the papacy.

Chapter 9 – The Seventh Crusade (1248–1254)

The peace brokered by Frederick in the Holy Land ended when Jerusalem was attacked by an army of Khwarezmians. These Sunni Muslim Turks had been forced out of their lands in Central Asia and Iran by invading Mongols. In the face of the collapse of their empire, the Khwarezmians moved south, seeking an alliance with Egyptian Mamluks. On the way, they laid siege to Jerusalem and occupied it in August 1244. They killed all but 2,000 of the inhabitants who remained in the city, leveling their defenses and buildings.

While the European Christians were simultaneously winning Spain and losing the Holy Land, a new scourge to security arose in the east. The enormous empire founded by the Mongol Genghis Khan and expanded by his sons and grandsons after his death in 1227 stretched from the Pacific Ocean to the shores of the Black Sea. Their westernmost conquests included Georgia, the Crimea, and Kievan Rus. These territories were the spoils of Batu Khan, a Mongol ruler and founder of the Golden Horde. The Mongols defeated the Kievan Rus nobles one by one, including the ruler of the principality of Vladimir-Suzdal, which included Moscow. The safety of the territory was guaranteed by the turning over of a young prince, Alexander Yaroslavich, to Batu as a hostage. Young Alexander absorbed the culture of the court of the Golden Horde, married a daughter of Batu Khan, and was placed as a Mongol prince in Novgorod where he defended the Mongols from the Swedes and the Germans. In the Battle of the Neva in July 1240, he trounced the Swedes, and for his military skill, he was given the sobriquet "Nevsky." Less than two years later, he repelled another invasion, this time a combined German-Latvian force who was routed in the Battle of the Ice. While Nevsky was thriving as a surrogate Mongol warrior, Batu laid siege to Kiev in December 1240. He then moved on into Poland, Hungary, and Transylvania and south into Croatia. The Mongols planned to follow up on their successes with an all-out attack on Germany, Austria, and Italy. In anticipation of his future military success in Europe, Batu demanded that Holy Roman Emperor Frederick II resign. The Mongol threat was sufficient for Pope Gregory IX to call for a Crusade against them. Central Europe escaped the Mongol invasion as the scourge from the East withdrew in 1242 to deal with issues of succession.

The Crusaders had a complicated relationship with the Mongols in the Levant. First, they allowed the Mamluks to move unhindered along their territory to defeat the Mongols at the Battle of Ain Jalut in 1260. But the Europeans soon changed tactics and enlisted the Mongols as allies in their fight against the Muslims. In the process of forming an alliance, the pope wrote to Mongol leaders encouraging them to convert to Western Christianity. This was not a completely unrealistic idea since a number of Mongols in the court were Nestorian Christians, members of a heretical Early Christian sect that had survived in the Persian Empire and the various Muslim dynasties that ruled the Persian Plateau, which was now entirely in the hands of the Mongols. A civil war in the Mongol Empire put an end to their abilities to fight as allies of the Christians.

In the Middle Ages, Europeans were fascinated with their co-religionist, albeit heretical, Nestorians and with the Mongols. A forged letter said to have been written to Byzantine Emperor Manuel I Komnenos in the 12th century by Prester John, a legendary elder of an early Christian group called the Nestorians who, it was said, disappeared in India. The letter told of the wonders of the East and Nestorian Christianity. The legend of Prester John was so ingrained into the minds of Europeans that it was held that a descendant of Prester John, King David of India, was headed to the Kingdom of Jerusalem and that he would relieve it from the Muslim threat. The confusion between a supposed Asian Christian nation and the very real Mongols existed. Prester John became identified with Genghis Khan's foster father, Toghrul, and he was also attributed to have extraordinary powers. The myth was in large part deflated with the reports of European travelers, such as the Franciscan brothers, Giovanni da Pian del Carpine and William of Rubruck, who both visited the court of the Great Khan at Karakorum. Carpine's book *Ystoria Mongalorum* written in the 1240s, the oldest of European accounts of the Mongols, was followed by Rubruck's account, which he presented to Louis IX in 1253. An even more detailed description of the wonders of the East was written by Marco Polo, who spent 24 years traveling in Asia with his father and uncle. After his return home, Marco Polo, while in service with the Venetians in their conflict with Genoa, was captured at sea and imprisoned. He dictated the account of his adventures in the East to his fellow inmate, Rustichello da Pisa, an Italian writer of romances. Marco Polo's *Travels* was copied over and over again in manuscript form and was read widely throughout Europe from the 14th century on.

With inaccurate information on the Mongols spreading across the lands, the Europeans began to fear them as much as the Muslims in the Levant. A pleading missive for reinforcements went out from the few remaining Christian cities in the Holy Land. The loss of Jerusalem to the Khwarezmians in 1244 and the potential outcome of the Mongols overrunning the Holy Land indicated that without immediate aid, the Christian presence in the Holy Land would be in great jeopardy. Fortunately, King Louis IX of France, commonly known as Saint Louis, had already taken the cross. Louis convened a group of his nobles in Paris in October 1245. Most agreed to follow him on the overseas venture, and he imposed a substantial tax to pay for the Crusade.

Recognizing that the only way to save the Holy Land was to destroy the Egyptians, Louis, his knights, and fighting men set sail in 1248, wintering in Cyprus. After receiving a desperate request for aid from Bohemond V, Prince of Antioch, Louis dispatched 500 knights to help in defense of the Christian principality.

In May, Louis and his remaining force, which numbered about 2,700 knights, 5,000 crossbowmen, and 7,300 foot soldiers, sailed from Cyprus to Damietta. Landing on the beach, the Crusaders were attacked by Muslims, but their discipline held, and they forced the Egyptians to retreat and give up their outpost at Damietta. It was Louis' plan to spend the summer taking the fortified city, but the quick victory required him to reschedule his invasion as he did not want to move up the Nile until the flood season was over. Louis was one who learned from other's mistakes, and he was well aware that Pelagius had been stranded by the flooding Nile. To avoid the same fate, he settled down to await the end of summer. This itself was a risky undertaking. Fighting men tended to turn on each other in the absence of enemies. Disease was also rampant in crowded camps, and Crusader forces were always prone to losing men due to the departure of those who became disheartened, homesick, or ill.

In November, Louis led his troops south, moving up the Nile on the bank opposite the fortress at modern-day Al Manṣūra. When it came time to cross the Nile, the Crusaders were unable to construct an adequate bridge. Having been shown the location of a ford by a local Coptic Christian, they proceeded into the river. Many knights drowned in the crossing. Troops in the vanguard, under the command of Louis IX's brother, Robert of Artois, along with a contingent of Knights Templar and soldiers from England under Sir William Longespée (an illegitimate grandson of King Henry II), attacked the Egyptian camp a few kilometers from Al Manṣūra. The commanders of the Mamluk Turks, who were fighting alongside the forces of the Ayyubid sultan of Egypt, took command of the entire army defending the Nile Delta. Under their leaders, Faris ad-Din Aktai and Baibars al-Bunduqdari, they held off the Crusaders.

A picture of the kind of fighting that took place around Al Manṣūra is given by Jean of Joinville in his description of the Crusade in his *Life of Saint Louis*. The Crusader noble wrote that some 6,000 Turks attacked him and his knights.

> As soon as they saw us they came charging toward us, and killed Hugues de Trichâtel, Lord of Conflans, who was with me bearing a banner. I and my knights spurred on our horses and went to the rescue of Raoul de Wanou, another of my company, whom they had struck to the ground. As I was coming back, the Turks thrust at me with their lances. Under the weight of their attack my horse was brought to its knees, and I went flying forward over its ears. I got up as soon as ever I could, with my shield at my neck and sword in hand.

According to Joinville, his troops in retreating to a ruined house to await reinforcements were overrun. "A great body of Turks came rushing at us, bearing me to the ground and riding over my body, so that my shield went flying from my neck." When the Crusaders had scuttled into the house, the Turks struck again.

> Some of them got into the house and pricked us with their lances from above. My knights asked me to hold on to their horses' bridles, which I did, for fear the beasts should run away. Then they put up a vigorous defence against the

Turks, for which, I may say, they were afterwards highly praised.

During this incident, some of the Crusaders suffered serious wounds that Joinville described in detail. Frédérick de Loupe had a lance thrust between his shoulders, which made "so large a wound that the blood poured from his body as if from the bung-hole of a barrel." A blow from one of the enemy's swords landed in the middle of Érard de Siverey's face, cutting through his nose so that it was left dangling over his lips.

The few remaining Crusaders from the vanguard escaped to join Louis, who was encamped nearby. There, the Crusaders managed to fight off several Muslim attacks. In the standoff, Louis opened negotiations with his enemy, offering to trade Damietta for Jerusalem. As talks dragged on, conditions deteriorated in the Christians' camp. The Muslims, as they had done in the past, prevented supply boats from traveling up from Damietta. Disease and declining morale forced the Crusaders to evacuate. The dangers of sailing, riding, or walking down the Nile through Muslim territory proved deadly. Crusader ships were attacked, and the stragglers on land were killed, as were the sick and diseased in the transport vessels. In the final battle of the Seventh Crusade at the Battle of Fariskur on April 6, 1250, the French were overwhelmed. Many of the prisoners that were too weak to walk were killed outright, and some of the defeated knights who were healthy were offered the, almost cliched, choice between death or conversion to Islam. Louis IX himself was captured along with his two brothers, Count Charles of Anjou and Count Alphonse of Poitiers. They were imprisoned in the house of the Egyptian royal chancellor at Al Manṣūra. Louis IX's brothers were eventually released and sent to France to secure the funds for a huge ransom for the king that was demanded by the Egyptians. Louis IX himself was tied in chains and shorn of his hair.

In France, there was, according to some with special affection for Louis IX, insufficient interest in raising his ransom. One of the outpourings of support came from a group of peasants; they were followers of an old Hungarian monk who they called the Master. He claimed to have been told by the Virgin Mary to enlist shepherds to join him in a mission to rescue the king. His Shepherds' Crusade of 1251 was said to have included 60,000 young men and women from Flanders and northern France. The enormous throng descended on Paris, where they entreated the regent Queen Blanche of Castile, Louis IX's mother, to support their cause. A contemporary ecclesiastical writer, Matthew Paris, viewed the Master as an imposter and that he was really one of the leaders of the Children's Crusade of 1212. Having no effect on the royal household, the shepherds rampaged throughout the north of France, causing serious harm, attacking priests and monasteries and even expelling the Archbishop of Rouen and attacking Jews in Amiens and Bourges. They were, in time, rounded up and excommunicated, and the Master was killed in a fight near Bourges.

While the Shepherds' Crusade was going on, the Knights Templar arranged for a sum of 400,000 dinars to be transported to Egypt, thus paying Louis IX's ransom. The French king on his release sailed to Acre. His arrival there was described by Joinville. "All the clergy and the people of that city came down to the sea-shore in procession, to meet him and welcome him with very great rejoicing." King Louis spent four years there using monies from his treasury to rebuild the defenses of Acre, Caesarea, and Jaffa. In the spring of 1254, he and his army returned to France. When he went home in 1254, he left behind well-manned garrisons which he himself financed from the annual royal income.

The defeat of the French Crusaders at Al Manṣūra was principally owing to the military skill of Baibars al-Bunduqdari. He was a Mamluk Turk in service of Sultan Turanshah of Egypt, who was the great-great nephew of Saladin. After the defeat of the

French, the Ayyubid sultan, who had come from Cairo, mistreated his faithful Mamluk soldiers and their leaders. The Mamluks revolted and killed the sultan.

Baibars, having proved himself to be an exemplary military leader in Egypt, marched with his army north to join a rival Mamluk warrior, Saif ad-Din Qutuz, in confronting the Mongols. The Mongols, who in their expansionist move to take over the world had sacked Baghdad and were now moving westward, had captured Aleppo and Damascus and threatened to attack Egypt itself. In the Battle of Ain Jalut in September of 1260 on the plains south of Nazareth, Qutuz and Baibars routed the Mongols. The Mamluks then retook Damascus and other Syrian cities. Qutuz did not get to savor his victory for, on his return to Cairo, he was assassinated. Baibars became the fourth in the Mamluk dynasty of sultans of Egypt.

Having put down an attempt to reinstate the Ayyubid rule in Cairo, Baibars then dealt with a fellow Mamluk, Emir Sinjar al-Halabi, who had occupied Damascus. After defeating him, Sultan Baibars turned to restore Egyptian control of Syria.

In 1263, Baibars attacked the city of Acre, the nominal capital of the Kingdom of Jerusalem. He was unsuccessful, so he turned to Nazareth. Using siege engines, the favored military machine of the Crusaders, his army breached the walls. He raised the citadel of Nazareth, and when he captured Haifa, he did the same. Afterward, Baibars besieged Arsuf. Baibars offered to release the captured Knights Hospitallerss if they agreed to abandon the city. They opted to accept the offer, but Baibars reneged and captured them. Baibars continued his successful invasion of the Levant. He forced the surrender of Antioch, razing the city, massacring much of the population, and selling the remaining people into slavery. At Jaffa, he repeated the process as he did subsequently at Ashkelon and Caesarea.

Chapter 10 – The Eighth Crusade (1270)

The successes of Baibars in the 1260s in the Holy Land rightly alarmed the Europeans to such an extent that the King of France, Louis IX, then in his fifties, decided to launch another Crusade. He formally took the cross on March 24, 1267. Louis and his army set sail from the Provence port of Aigues-Mortes in the summer of 1270. His departure had been preceded by a Spanish contingent that departed from Barcelona under King James I of Aragon in the fall of 1269. The Aragonese flotilla was damaged by a storm, and most of the survivors returned to Spain, but a small contingent did struggle to Acre where they engaged with Baibars' troops. Unable to dislodge the Egyptian sultan, they returned home.

Louis IX abandoned his initial plan to sail to Cyprus and then on to the Holy Land. Instead, he chose to sail south to Tunis in North Africa, where he hoped to subdue the city by converting the caliph to Christianity and thus interrupt the forwarding of supplies to Egypt, weakening Baibars' sultanate.

Louis' forces were augmented by one provided by the King of Navarre, which sailed from Marseille. Both met off Sardinia and then proceeded to the coast of Tunisia. The arrival of the English fleet carrying Crusaders was delayed as Henry III of England, who had agreed to participate, backed out and sent his son Prince Edward instead.

After reaching North Africa, the Crusaders set up camp near Carthage. While awaiting reinforcements, they fell victim to a virulent epidemic of dysentery. Louis himself died of the disease on August 25, 1270. The Crusaders, after making a treaty with the caliph of Tunis, prepared to evacuate from North Africa. While most of the French troops returned home, Prince Edward of England took his army of about 1,000 men, including 225 knights, to Acre, where he disembarked on May 9, 1271.

The Ninth Crusade (1271-1272)

This Crusade is sometimes considered to be a part of the Eighth Crusade (which is why it does not have its own chapter), and it is commonly seen as the last Crusade to reach the Holy Land before the fall of Acre in 1291.

Hearing of the failure of Louis IX's Crusade in North Africa and the death of the king himself, the Mamluk Sultan Baibars rescinded his orders to his generals in Cairo to march westward to relieve Tunis. He continued to lay siege to Crusader castles in Syria during this time. At the seemingly impregnable Krak des Chevaliers, Baibars' army breached the outer walls in two days. They did this by using mangonels modeled after those of the Crusaders. Baibars then concocted a clever plan to force the defenders to surrender by sending them a forged letter. Purported to be from the Grand Master of the Knights Hospitallers, the letter instructed the Hospitallers stationed there to surrender. After a lull in fighting that lasted ten days, the Hospitallers, in early April 1271, negotiated their departure from Krak des Chevaliers, and their lives were spared.

The loss of Krak des Chevaliers was a blow to the Hospitallers. It was believed that the enormous castle was impregnable, and it had been the finest and largest of the Hospitallers' castles along the border of the County of Tripoli. In the mid-13th century, this outpost was defended by about 2,000 troops. The castle was surrounded by two concentric walls, and the three-meter-thick inner wall had seven protective towers, each ten meters in diameter. The castle was supplied with an enormous storeroom containing food sufficient enough to sustain the defenders throughout a siege of five years. The stable held as many as 1,000 horses.

In 1271, Prince Edward assessed the situation from Acre, the last remaining Christian stronghold in the Holy Land. With insufficient forces to fend off an attack by Baibars, he sent an embassy to the Mongols to enlist their help. This they provided by attacking Baibars' city of Aleppo, distracting him for a while. With Baibars busy at Aleppo, Edward attempted to open up a route to Jerusalem. However, he failed in this endeavor. In May of 1272, Hugh III of Cyprus, the King of Jerusalem, signed a ten-year truce with Baibars in an attempt to alleviate pressure on Acre, thus ending the Ninth Crusade.

Prince Edward's Crusader career ended when he was attacked by a Muslim assassin. The heir to the throne of England killed his assailant but suffered a severe stab wound in his arm. He survived thanks to the ministrations of his wife, Eleanor of Castile, who had accompanied him on his Crusade. In poor health, Edward left Acre on September 24, 1272, sailing to Sicily, where he learned that his father, Henry III, had died in November 1272. Edward put off returning to England, and eventually, he moved with his courtly entourage north, stopping in Italy and France where he met with Pope Gregory X in the summer of 1274. He arrived in England on August 2, 1274, and was crowned two weeks later. Informed of the dire situation in the Holy Land, Pope Gregory X attempted to raise enthusiasm in Europe for another Crusade but it fell on deaf ears, possibly because the papacy had, for many years, used the call for a Crusade to deal with European enemies, both secular and religious, rather than the Muslims in the Holy Land. With no reinforcements on the horizon, the King of Jerusalem, Hugh III, moved his court to Cyprus in 1276. Although Baibars died in Damascus in July 1277, his successors continued to exert extreme pressure on the remaining Christian holdings in the Near East.

As the situation became even more dire in the Holy Land, Pope Nicholas IV, in 1289, tried in vain to inspire European kings and nobles to take the cross. His pleadings were unsuccessful as domestic conflicts distracted potential leaders of a Crusade.

In 1291, tensions around Acre, the last Crusader city in the Holy Land, came to a boil. A flotilla of Venetian galleys arrived with some 1,600 men. They were, according to some sources, ill-trained peasants and unemployed men from Tuscany and Lombardy. Upon disembarking, they attacked the Muslims in the vicinity of Acre. The Mamluk Sultan Al-Mansur Qalawun accused the Crusaders of breaching the treaty. He began mobilizing his forces for an all-out siege of Acre. Crusader peace negotiators sent to Cairo were ignored and imprisoned. Qalawun's son, who had succeeded his father as the Mamluk sultan of Egypt and Syria, marched against the Crusaders. He was reinforced by fighters from Damascus and other towns and cities in the Levant, as well as a large contingent of soldiers from Cairo who arrived at Acre on April 6, 1291. Over a period of several days, the Muslims succeeded in undermining the walls of the city while they rebuffed Crusader attempts to negotiate a peace. On May 18, the Muslims launched an all-out attack against the now breachable walls. Street fighting reduced the number of Christian defenders, and eventually, those that were still alive evacuated the city and fled on galleys to Cyprus.

The fall of Acre in 1291 signaled the end of Christian Crusading activities in the Holy Land.

Conclusion

The Aftermath: The Idea of Crusading Continues

In August of 1308, Pope Clement V called for faithful Christians to take the cross for another Crusade to be launched the following year. The pope's plan was for the Hospitallers to lead a limited expedition to the East. He asked that those who preached the Crusade ask for prayers from the laity and the donation of funds to support the Hospitallers. In exchange for financing the Crusade, the pope, following in the steps of his predecessors, offered donors indulgences, or advance absolution for their sins.

Those who preached the Crusade were remarkably successful in stirring up the peasantry. Although the lower classes were not, in fact, encouraged to take the cross, many of them in Northern Europe proceeded to sew a red cross on their garb, assemble en masse, and hasten off to the papal palace at Avignon to offer their service to the pope. These poor Crusaders, who styled themselves as the "Brothers of the Cross," supported themselves on their journey south by attacking Jewish communities they met along the way and looting their property. In Brabant, Jewish people took refuge in the castle of Duke John II. They were saved when he sent his army out to chase the poor Crusaders away.

In July 1309, the poor Crusaders, possibly as many as 40,000, arrived in Avignon and asked the pope to authorize a full-scale Crusade. He refused, and the Hospitallers refused to board any of them on the ships that the peasants believed would take them to the Holy Land. Without papal authorization and without transport, the poor Crusaders dispersed and returned to their homes.

In the spring of 1311, a fleet of galleys in Brindisi was prepared for the Hospitallers. They set out on an expedition to the East, which they called a Crusade. The ships, carrying from 200 to 300 knights and 3,000 foot soldiers, landed on the Greek island of Rhodes. It was, in fact, never the intention of the Hospitallers to proceed to the Holy Land. Their goal was to complete the conquest of the island and remove the last Byzantine soldiers from the city of Rhodes. The Crusade was thus not directed at Muslims but fellow Christians. On August 15, 1311, the Hospitallers captured the city of Rhodes. The order then transferred its convent and hospital from Cyprus to Rhodes and commenced operations against Venetian trading posts in the Aegean Sea, as well as engaging with the Turkish fleet. In a naval battle in 1319 near the island of Chios, the Hospitallers defeated the Turks and set in motion a push to end Muslim seaborne predation in the Aegean.

The idea of launching military expeditions under the cover of the word "Crusade" was slow to die out. The King of Cyprus, Peter I, who was nominally King of Jerusalem—a kingdom without any territory in the Holy Land—spent three years from 1362 to 1365 forming an army and soliciting financial support for a Crusade. His venture, under the guise of a religious operation, appears to have been motivated by economics, more specifically the termination of Alexandria's primacy as a trading port, rather than religious fervor.

In October 1365, Peter's forces sailed to Rhodes where they picked up some Hospitallers. With 165 ships, he then sailed to Alexandria, and on October 9, 1365, he launched a vicious attack on the city. The massacre of the population and the leveling of buildings was followed by a withdrawal so Peter could proceed farther into Egypt. His plan was cut short when the knights in his army refused to continue with the invasion, preferring to return home with their loot.

The gradual corruption of the notion of a Crusade is clear in the several so-called Crusades that were launched in Europe over the centuries following the fall of Acre in 1291. An example of this is the Crusade launched by Pope Urban VI against the supporters of the antipope in Avignon, Clement VII, who was elected into office by French cardinals. This was purely a European dispute and had nothing to do with the Holy Land. The leader of this so-called Crusade was the English Bishop of Norwich, Henry le Despenser. His army crossed the channel and besieged Ypres in 1383. A chronicler wrote that "having the banner of the Holy Cross before them...those who suffered death would be martyrs...and thus the blessing of the cross was achieved." Despenser's Crusade achieved nothing but death and destruction of fellow Christians. He abandoned the expedition and was subsequently impeached for his behavior.

This was not the end of the Church calling for Crusades against dissidents. On March 17, 1420, Pope Martin V issued a bull imploring the faithful to join in destroying dissident Christians or heretics belonging to the Wycliffite and Hussite sects in Bohemia. The Hussites were followers of the theologian Jan Hus, who was influenced by the writings of John Wycliffe and who was excommunicated by the Catholic Church and then burnt at the stake in 1415 for his heretical views on the presence of the body of Christ in Holy Communion. The King of Hungary, Germany, and Bohemia, Sigismund of Luxembourg, responding to Pope Martin's call for Crusade and assembled a large army of European knights and laid siege to the city of Prague, then the center of the Hussite rebellion against canonical Catholicism. Sigismund's Crusade was halted with a series of battlefield victories by the Hussites beginning in 1420. Four more calls by the papacy for Crusades against the Hussites failed to result in a victory of the Catholic Church over the Bohemian heretics. While some of those who took the cross in the struggle against the Hussites may have been genuinely motivated by a desire to protect the canonical doctrines of the Church, most of the knights and indeed Sigismund himself were driven by purely secular intentions—Sigismund to expand his power and the knights to increase their wealth through looting.

The decline of enthusiasm for Crusades by European leaders was a result of the evolution of medieval society following the fall of Acre in 1291 that occurred after the Ninth Crusade. Crusading was an expensive undertaking, and funds for adventuring in the Near East became more and more difficult to obtain. Such finances that could be raised for war were more effectively spent pursuing territorial expansion in Europe itself.

With the rise in power of independent city-states in Italy and proto-democratic urban centers in northern Europe, there was a gradual transference of power from aristocratic noble families, whose wealth was derived from agriculture, to urban merchant families. The notion of knightly honor slowly became fossilized so that it was acted out in tournaments, which were far less dangerous than fighting in a far-off land against unpredictable enemies using unpredictable tactics and more and more effective weapons. Wars did occur in Europe, and there were many, which typically tended to be internecine struggles or civil wars. The authority of the papacy also gradually declined as the Church became embroiled in struggles against heretical sects and eventually various forms of Protestantism.

In sum, the Crusades offered a religiously justified adventure for European knights and common folk. When successful, the lands acquired in the Near East by the Crusader knights were insufficient to support a stable noble lifestyle. Not only were the incomes derived from the estates in the East negligible as compared to what could be expected on European soil, but their defense was also extraordinarily costly in terms of lives and money. Without a long-term guarantee of subsidies from Europe, the Crusader knights were incapable of holding their estates and defending the Kingdom of Jerusalem. The arrival of the Mongols in Europe resulted in the expansion of their empire, which lasted from 1236 to 1242, and included most of Eastern Europe, then much of the Balkans, and later Anatolia; this just meant that there was yet another danger to be faced in the East. The idea of Crusading in the Holy Land became more and more impractical in terms of victory on the battlefield by European soldiers. If anything, the Crusades proved that there was no place for Europeans in the Levant.

Part 2: The Silk Road

A Captivating Guide to the Ancient Network of Trade Routes Established during the Han Dynasty of China and How It Connected the East and West

Introduction

Trade in goods necessarily carries with it trade in ideas. In other words, ideas piggy-back on the transmission of mercantile goods. It is through this means that religions, concepts of organization of societies, art, and material culture are transmitted from one society to another.

The development of civilizations and the enrichment of different cultures depend on trade between each other. Without trade and the transference of ideas, without vibrant cultures distinguished by religion and technology meeting with each other in the marketplace, civilizations fossilize and eventually decline. In some cases, they may even disappear. It is the impetus of the new that maintains the robust evolution of civilizations and cultures. Without new ideas impinging on them, civilizations and cultures are incapable of adapting to change and lose their vitality in an ever-changing world.

European civilizations and Asian civilizations, in particular, Chinese civilization, from roughly 100 BCE to 1450 CE, depended on interconnections through trade to evolve. This trade was carried out along what is known to us as the Silk Road.

The Silk Road, transformative for both Asian and European cultures and civilizations, owes its name and identity to modern scholars, among whom are archaeologists, linguists, economists, geographers, and historians. What we call the Silk Road today was actually named by the German explorer Ferdinand von Richthofen in 1877. He identified the Silk Road (Seidenstrasse) as a continuous land route along which trade was carried out, beginning in the era of imperial Rome and the Han Dynasty in China (206 BCE–220 CE). Von Richthofen's travels and discoveries, as well as his readings of the 2nd-century texts of the Greek geographer Ptolemy and the 1st-century writings of the Roman Pliny the Elder, convinced him that there was once a defined road from the Near East to central China along which silk was transported. According to von Richthofen, silk was the prime luxury good.

Von Richthofen's student, Swedish geographer Sven Hedin, undertook four expeditions to central Asia in the late 19th and early 20th centuries, mapping and observing the cultures of the various peoples he met along the way. His discoveries, in large measure, confirmed the notion that a Silk Road existed and that trade between the East and the West had been carried out for centuries in the distant past. Hedin reported on his travels in central Asia in multivolume technical reports. He summarized his research in a more popular book that made his work more accessible to the general public. This book, first published in Swedish in 1936 and was translated into English in 1938 under the title *The Silk Road*, inaugurated what was to become a worldwide fascination with the subject, a fascination that still persists today. Sven Hedin identified Chang'an (modern-day Xi'an), the Han dynasty capital, as the eastern end of the Silk Road, which he said terminated in the West some 7,000 kilometers (almost 4,350 miles) away in Antioch, Syria.

The idea of a Silk Road has, since the days of von Richthofen and Hedin, captured the imagination of the public. Starting in the 1960s, there was a flood of books, both scholarly and popular, published on the subject. The opening of China for archaeological research by non-Chinese scholars in the late 1970s increased public enthusiasm in the West as well. With the introduction of prohibitions against the plundering of archaeological sites, something that in the past had led to the dispersion of art and cultural treasures from China and central Asia to European and American museums, those who were enchanted by the idea of the Silk Road began to travel to previously out-of-bounds cities and towns situated along what was popularly known as the Silk Road. Interest in the trade route between the East and the West increased with the dissolution of the Soviet Union in 1991, as it opened up more Silk Road sites in Central Asia for study and exploration by tourists and scholars. The whole enterprise of study and exploitation of sites along the Silk Road has since became ensnared in the politics of bridging the histories of Eastern and Western civilizations. The notions of connecting the cultures of the East and the West has become a common topic in contemporary Silk Road studies. In recent years, the Eurocentric approach to world history has begun to crumble as more and more scholars from all regions of Asia have promoted a wider non-Eurocentric understanding of the histories of nations and cultures that once were of little interest in the West before.

The idea that exotic goods from the East, primarily silk, were transported thousands of miles across deserts and over mountains on long trains of camels, however picturesque and romantic, has proved to be untrue. With the increasing sophistication of archaeology and the interpretation of ancient texts by Eastern and Western scholars, a much more complicated picture of the Silk Road has emerged. It is now clear that the Silk Road was not a single, distinct avenue of trade but rather a complex series of paths connecting small communities and larger urban settlements in central Asia. Along these paths, objects of trade were moved by small caravans. So, contrary to popular belief, traders did not travel great distances. Objects from the East and the West were handed off from one middleman to another. Some goods did move all the way from central China to Rome, and later medieval Europe, but most of the trade was local, taking place between adjacent cultures or peoples. The variety of goods that moved short and long distances from the East to the West or vice versa were much more mundane than the silk that was thought to be so highly prized in the West. However, something that was not so mundane was the transmission of ideas along the trade routes that comprised the Silk Road. It was along this assortment of paths that religions, such as Buddhism, Islam, and Christianity, made inroads among the populations of central Asia and eventually China.

The enormous interest in the Silk Road has spawned a lively debate among researchers, whose numbers have increased exponentially with contributions from Chinese scholars and researchers in modern nations along the East-West trade routes. The globalization of academic work on the Silk Road is exemplified by the establishment of international centers for cooperative research, such as the Institute of Silk Road Studies in Kamakura, Japan, founded in 1990; the Central Asia-Caucasus Institute and Silk Road Studies Program, founded in Washington in 1996; and the Tang Centre for Silk Road Studies at the University of California, which was established in 2017. Among the research papers currently being published on the subject by these and other research centers, there is a notable abundance of scholarly articles questioning whether there was indeed a Silk Road. It has even been called "a romantic deception" and "the road that never was."

The concept of a singular Silk Road has been subject to revision, and it is now questioned whether East-West trade from Roman times to the 15th century involved much silk at all. Further, the notion of a single road has been replaced with the identification of a multiplicity of routes, which are more accurately called paths than roads. There is a great debate on which trade routes to include under the umbrella of the term "Silk Road." Some scholars are proponents of adding sea routes between south Asia and the West, and others conclude that the trade route from India through the Karakoram mountain range on the borders of Pakistan, India, and China cannot be excluded from Silk Road studies. Several contemporary scholars have also proposed that sea and land routes connecting Africa with the East belong in the realm of Silk Road studies.

The Silk Road, which has been understood as a generalized route of trade between the East and the West, is different from European, North African, and Near Eastern trade routes because until recently, it has been understood as solely being a land route; in fact, it was believed to be the longest overland trade route in human history. From pre-Roman times to the Railway Age in Europe, most of the trade within Europe was conducted by seas or rivers. Trade from the north to the south was facilitated by the existence of the long navigable rivers of Europe, such as the Danube, Rhine, and Volga, or by sea from the Mediterranean through the Atlantic Ocean to the North Sea and then the Baltic. European trade with North Africa and the Near East depended almost entirely on the Mediterranean Sea routes. Trade with India and beyond into Southeast Asia involved short overland transportation to centers where goods were transferred to ships plying the Indian Ocean. In contrast to this was the Silk Road, where vast stretches of often inhospitable land lay between trading entrepots. For this reason, it has captured the imagination of students of history, geography, and the transmission of culture.

Because the Silk Road was not a single path from China to the Near East but instead consisted of a network of shorter connected routes, the complexities of the terrain and cultures along the routes pose greater problems to understanding its history than trade routes that involved long-distance sea transportation. Near Eastern and Mediterranean ports are, by a straight line, 8,500 kilometers (almost 5,282 miles) distant from Xi'an, the ancient capital of China. The complicated topography of central Asia required traders to detour around impassable mountain ranges and traverse deserts from one oasis to another, as well as to contend with disruptions due to warfare between tribes and proto-nations. All of this would make the total distance between the East and the West much longer.

The routes of East/West trade were such that they encompassed a wide range of peoples or cultures that inhabited central Asia. These peoples lived in the modern nations of China, Kyrgyzstan, Tajikistan, Kazakhstan, Uzbekistan, Turkmenistan, Afghanistan, Iran, and Iraq. Over the history of the Silk Road, the cultures that were involved in the movement of goods across central Asia changed as they were subject to invasions by displaced nomadic tribes and conquest by superior imperial powers. Thus, the complicated history of the Silk Road involves the history of peoples and geography that is better understood by local scholars and is, more often than not, completely beyond the knowledge of others outside the region. In effect, the understanding of the Silk Road among Europeans is almost as foggy as the Romans' comprehension of what lay in the East beyond the borders of their empire.

For the Europeans from Roman times to the 15th century and beyond, there existed a fascination for the exotic, unknown cultures and products of the East. From the evidence available, it seems as if there was not an equivalent fascination for Western culture among the Chinese. For the most part, the Chinese looked to the West, central Asia, and later as far as the Near East and Europe as a straightforward market for goods or, in short, a source of wealth.

European interest in the East can be traced back to the remarkable expansion of the Hellenistic Greek Empire under Alexander the Great. His military incursions into Asia, through Persia and modern-day Afghanistan, to the banks of the Indus River became the stuff of legend, and it drove Europeans to imagine the magnificence of mysterious Eastern civilizations. In expanding his empire to the East, Alexander planted outposts of Greek culture. These outposts or garrisons became centers for the transmission of ideas and goods of Eastern cultures into the ancient Greek and Roman worlds and vice versa. The importance of these outposts for the transmission of culture is represented by the existence of locally made ancient artworks excavated in Iran, Iraq, and Afghanistan that are stylistically related to the Hellenistic art of the Macedonian world of Alexander the Great.

The history of the Silk Road is extremely complex. It cannot be told as a singular chronological narrative. Different cultures and societies rose and vanished along the Silk Road, and peoples migrated from one region to another. In short, for most of its history, there was fluidity as to the dominant cultures along the route or routes. Explaining the rise and fall or disappearance of these cultures involves stopping along the way to consider the chronology of their histories.

Chapter 1 – Rome, Silk, and Ancient Geography

The establishment of the earliest western terminus of the Silk Road has been based on the supposition that Chinese silk was among the major luxuries consumed by wealthy Romans. It has been thought that in the era of the late Roman Republic, which ended in 27 BCE, Chinese silk passed through Parthian merchants to be consumed by Roman patricians. However, it has been convincingly proved that silk available in the Roman markets, lasting well into the imperial period, was woven in western Asia, specifically in Damascus and Mosul. This has been proved by the analysis of the thread; it is distinctly of the type produced by species of silkworms that were raised in western and central Asia.

Many people may not realize that silk is produced in different ways, and since silk was thought to be the most popular item on the Silk Road, it is worth delving into the different ways silk was made. There was also a source for silk in the Indian subcontinent, where the fabric had been produced since around 2500 BCE. Silk produced in India and on the Aegean island of Cos in the 1ˢᵗ century, as well as earlier, was made from cocoons that were naturally vacated by moths. The silk thread was then scraped from the cocoons. In China, however, the method of production of the thread was different. By as early as 4000 BCE, the silk moth was domesticated in China. Here, the cocoons were boiled with the pupae inside. Long strands of silk thread were pulled from the damp cocoons and then woven into fabrics.

The Romans called the producers of silk the people of Seres, a designation derived from the ancient name Serica, which was one of the easternmost countries known to the ancient Greeks and Romans. This does not mean, as early writers on the Silk Road have assumed, what is modern-day China. It merely referred to the origins of silk that was used in Rome. The *Periplus of the Erythrean Sea*, a Greek language maritime guidebook that was written in the 1ˢᵗ century, describes ports on the Red Sea, Africa, the Persian Gulf, and India, as well as mentions lands beyond the known world. "Somewhere on the outer fringe, there is a very great inland city called Thina [or Sinae] from which silk floss, yarn, and cloth are shipped by land...and via the Ganges River." The anonymous author said, "It is not easy to get to this Thina: for rarely do people come from it." This rendering of Thina was based on the information the writer received from Indian traders.

More information on Roman consumption of silk is available in the writings of Pliny the Elder, who lived from 23 to 70 CE. He was confused about the method in which silk was produced. He thought it was made from white down that adhered to leaves. This down, he thought incorrectly, was scraped off to make silk thread. This description is closer to the production of cotton than that of silk. Pliny, in another passage, noted that the silk worn by Roman women was difficult to manufacture and came from a distant land. He objected to it because it allowed "the Roman matron to flaunt transparent raiment in public."

Because it is difficult to identify the source of silk thread, it is not entirely clear where all of the surviving fragments of Roman silk garments originated. The decorative motifs that were woven into the fabric, when they seem to be of Chinese origin, may instead be Indian copies of Chinese designs. The most certain way to prove a fabric found in the West came from China is the presence of Chinese characters woven into the cloth. Textiles unearthed in Palmyra, Syria, are the earliest Chinese fabrics, complete with decorative Chinese characters, that have been found in the West. They date from the 1st to the 3rd centuries CE. More abundant samples of silk fabrics have survived from the Byzantine Empire from the 5th to the 15th centuries. The analysis of around one thousand samples has revealed only a single one that can be identified as Chinese, although there is some evidence that the Byzantines during the reign of Emperor Justinian I, who ruled from 527 to 565 CE, acquired Chinese silk through trade with people of an ancient Iranian culture called the Sogdians.

It was a Byzantine scholar, Cosmas Indicopleustes, who was the first Westerner to write about China. In his *Christian Topography*, dating from about 550 CE, he used the name Tzinista to designate an East Asian country that was called by its inhabitants as Zhōngguó (*zhōng* meaning middle and *guó* meaning state). Later, the Romans used Taugast as the name for China. It was the name commonly used among Turkic peoples of central Asia to designate the country to their east. A historian during the reign of Byzantine Emperor Heraclius (r. 610-641) adopted this name in his writing.

For their part, the Chinese had only unclear ideas of what lay beyond central Asia. There are references to Egypt but not to Rome in the *Weilüe*, a Chinese historical text composed sometime between 239 and 265 CE. In what is known as the *Book of the Later Han*, compiled sometime between 398 and 445 CE, the descriptions of the lands farthest west seem to be those of the Near East, in particular, Iran and Syria. Later Chinese texts from the 8th century again mention the Near East and refer to Constantinople but are silent on any places in greater Europe.

The first encounter between the Chinese and the Romans may have taken place in the early 1st century. It was reported by the 2nd-century historian Florus that during the reign of Augustus (r. 27 BCE–14 CE), among the many delegations from the East were people called Seres. Because this event is not recorded in any other history, it probably did not occur. From Chinese records, it is likely that the envoy Gan Ying was the first to travel west in a mission to the Roman Empire. In 97 CE, he got as far as Mesopotamia, where he intended to sail west. He was advised that the journey was dangerous and long, so he returned to China without seeing the Mediterranean or Rome itself.

If trade had been established in the era of the Roman Empire before the Sack of Rome in 410, one would expect that Roman coins would have turned up in archaeological sites in the East. To date, no ancient Roman coins have been found in China. The earliest Western coins found were all minted in Byzantium dating from the first half of the 6th century CE. It is important to note that along the southwest coast of India, thousands of Roman gold and silver coins have turned up in archaeological excavations. This indicates that significant maritime and overland trade existed between Rome and India. Also, Roman coins have appeared in what is today Vietnam, suggesting that maritime trade between Rome and Southeast Asia predated any land-based commerce between Europe and the Far East.

To summarize, the evidence in the West suggests that it was only sometime after the 1st century CE, at the earliest, that any trade existed between areas in the eastern provinces of the Roman Empire, such as Syria, and the Far East. Clearly, the Romans did not know of the existence of China until much later.

In terms of Western names for the great land of the Far East, the term China was adopted by the English in the 16th century from the Portuguese. Scholars have traced its origin to Persian or possibly Sanskrit. It is more likely derived from the word Qin, the Chinese name of the Qin dynasty, which lasted from 221 to 206 BCE. It was during the Qin dynasty that the various peoples of China were first united under a central government.

Chapter 2 – Han Silk Production and Trade

China's first imperial dynasty, the Qin, was replaced by the Han Dynasty, which rose to power with the Han people dominating in a period of warring ethnic factions contending for power. The first Han emperor, Liu Bang, who reigned from 202 to 195 BCE, succeeded in the pacification of eighteen feudal states, forming a dominion of what consists of part of modern-day China under his rule. He established the capital of the Han Chinese state at Chang'an, modern-day Xi'an. In the early years of the Han dynasty, soldiers were dispatched to the frontiers to protect the empire from barbarian incursions on the frontiers. In order to diminish the frequency of raids by peoples outside Han China, border markets were opened so that those living outside the Han Empire, beyond walled fortifications, could carry out regulated trade with Han merchants. This method of pacification became the Han norm in order to expand influence, as well as to encourage trade. In the wake of organized trade, the Han, through force, could assimilate peoples on the frontier and eventually feed the imperial treasury with income derived from taxation.

The Han policy of establishing regulated trade with peoples beyond the frontiers of their empire required obtaining knowledge of these peoples, of which there were many, what surplus goods they had, and what goods they wished to acquire from the Chinese. The seventh emperor of the Han dynasty, Emperor Wu (r. 141 BCE–87 BCE) in 138 BCE dispatched an envoy named Zhang Qian to form an alliance with nomadic pastoralists called the Yuezhi people who moved into Sogdia in the 2nd century BCE, a loose confederation of indigenous peoples located in what is present-day Kazakhstan, Tajikistan, and Uzbekistan.

Before the arrival of the Yuezhi, the Sogdians had a centuries-old culture that was shaped by their history of conquest by Near Eastern and Mediterranean empires. The Sogdians were ruled first by Persian Cyrus the Great (r. 559 BCE–530 BCE), and then their lands were annexed by Alexander the Great in 328 BCE. The Sogdian confederation of tribes was centered on the city of Samarkand. After the death of Alexander the Great, Sogdia became a part of the Greek Seleucid Empire and then a part of the Greco-Bactrian Kingdom, which extended from northern Iran to the Hindu Kush mountain range and as far as the Oxus River.

The initiation of trade with the Yuezhi was not the only motive for Wu's emissary Zhang Qian's mission. It was his intention to enlist the Yuezhi as Han allies in a battle against the Xiongnu of Mongolia and the Manchurian steppe, which was a menacing threat to the Han Empire on the northern frontier. The Xiongnu was a confederation of nomadic tribes that were united as the Xiongnu Empire under Modu, who ruled from 209 BCE to 174 BCE. Modu's warriors were constantly warring with peoples to the east of the Han Empire and peoples in the west, including the Yuezhi. Like with all movements and aggression by barbarian tribes, the result was the pushing of weaker tribes into new regions. The pressure on these weaker tribes meant that they moved into areas occupied by other tribes and displacing them. This constant tribal migration upset trade and inflicted pressure on settled people like the Han.

The wars between the Xiongnu and neighboring peoples continued after Modu's death. As such, it was into an area of unsettled tribal supremacy that Zhang Qian traveled in.

Unfortunately, the diplomat was captured by the Xiongnu in 138 BCE, and they enslaved him for ten years. After escaping, Zhang Qian finally made contact with the Yuezhi, who pastured their livestock to the west of where the Xiongnu were settled. Zhang eventually had to report back to the Han emperor that any alliance with the Yuezhi was not to be, as the Yuezhi showed no interest in fighting against their de facto overlords, the Xiongnu.

Zhang Qian was more successful as an explorer than as a diplomat. His reports of his travels among the peoples of central Asia convinced Han authorities that beyond the frontiers of their empire lay opportunities for the expansion of trade and perhaps tribute through taxation. In his travels, Zhang met the inhabitants of Dayuan, which was an urban center in the Fergana Valley in central Asia that stretched across today's eastern Uzbekistan, southern Kyrgyzstan, and northern Tajikistan. Dayuan was 1,500 kilometers (around 932 miles) from the Han capital of Chang'an. Zhang Qian reported that the residents of Dayuan had Caucasian features, lived in walled cities, were consumers of wine, and raised remarkably hardy horses. Zhang tried unsuccessfully to convince the people of Dayuan to send some of their extraordinary horses to Emperor Wu.

The culture of the people of Dayuan was quite different from the cultures of the nomadic peoples who surrounded them, among which were the Yuezhi. The Fergana Valley had been conquered by Alexander the Great in 329 BCE, where he founded the city of Alexandria Eschate (Alexandria the Furthest) on the banks of the Syr Darya River on the site of the present-day city of Khujand, Tajikistan. Upon the death of Alexander, his walled city fell under the control of the Seleucid Empire and then became a part of the Greco-Bactrian Kingdom. According to the Greek historian Strabo (63 BCE–24 CE), the Greco-Bactrians expanded their kingdom "as far as the Seres [Chinese] and the Phryni," a generic term for the people of the Far East. There is archaeological evidence of late Hellenistic-inspired statuettes of Greek soldiers that indicates the Greco-Bactrians may have penetrated as far east as modern-day Ürümqi in the Chinese region of Xinjiang.

The Greco-Bactrian Kingdom was founded in 250 BCE when a secessionist Seleucid leader set himself up as King Diodotus I Soter of Bactria. His successor, Diodotus II, was overthrown by the Greek Euthydemus, who, between 210 and 220 BCE, expanded the Greco-Bactrian Kingdom, moving as far east as Xinjiang (modern northwestern China). The Greek historian Strabo wrote that "they [the Greco-Bactrians] extended their empire even as far as the Seres [the Chinese]." The Greco-Bactrians also expanded their sway south under King Demetrius I (r. circa 200 BCE–180 BCE), who successfully annexed modern-day Afghanistan, Pakistan, Punjab, and parts of the Indian subcontinent.

When the diplomat Zhang Qian arrived in Dayuan in about 128 BCE, he saw warriors demonstrate shooting arrows from horseback. This suggests that the residents were, at the time, nomadic herdsmen who had migrated to the city to seek the protection of the Greco-Bactrian Kingdom, which was then being invaded by the Yuezhi. The Yuezhi were being pushed out of their pasture lands by expanding tribes of nomadic pastoralists. The migrating Yuezhi bypassed Dayuan and practiced their nomadic life to the southwest, where they fought off the authority of the declining Greco-Bactrian Kingdom.

On his return east to China, Zhang Qian was again captured by the Xiongnu. He escaped in the midst of a civil war in the Xiongnu Empire and made his way home to Chang'an.

The history of Sogdia, where the Yuezhi eventually "settled," as much as the word can be applied to traditional nomads, is even more complicated. Its geographical location made it susceptible to the force of other migrant tribes following in their footsteps from both the east and the west. In the 1st century CE, Sogdia became the center of a new empire formed by the Yuezhi, who had lived in Bactria. The Kushan Empire extended from Sogdia in the north, through Afghanistan, and into northern India. Kushan Emperor Kanishka the Great (r. circa 127–150 CE), who was probably of Yuezhi ethnicity, reformed and expanded the empire, setting up capitals at Purusapura in the Peshawar Basin (located in modern-day Pakistan and Afghanistan) and Kapisi (near modern-day Bagram, Afghanistan). Kanishka also expanded his empire to the south, taking most of India. By connecting India with central Asia as far north as the Fergana Valley and as far east as Furfan, which was adjacent to the border of Han China, the Kushan Empire was able to efficiently trade north to south and fostered trade from Sogdia to China. It was along these trade routes of the Silk Road that Buddhism made its way from India, where Siddhartha Gautama, its founder, was born about 563 BCE. His teachings slowly spread into central Asia, and the religion reached China in the 2nd century CE, which is when Buddhist monks are first recorded as having translated their texts into Chinese.

Chapter 3 – The Kingdom of Loulan

The first successful concerted effort to expand trading toward the West by the Han emperors themselves began in the 1st century BCE. This mercantile venture was centered on the oasis city of Loulan, where a sophisticated kingdom had grown to dominate the region by the second century BCE.

In Chinese, Turkestan (which included part of modern-day Xinjiang), in what is now a sparsely inhabited wasteland, explorers and archaeologists have discovered a previously unknown ancient culture in what is designated today as the Shanshan Basin. Skirting the southern margins of the Taklamakan Desert, the Shanshan Basin has yielded spectacular archaeological discoveries. In the now desolate region, at the sites of the ancient cities of Niya and Loulan, archaeologists have discovered the remains of a sophisticated culture that had significant importance in connecting central Asia with cultures from the south as far as India.

Archaeological evidence has proved that the people who lived in the urban centers of Niya and Loulan were in regular contact with traders from the south. These southern merchants moved north through the mountain ranges of the Karakoram, Hindu Kush,

Pamir, Kunlun, and Himalayas. Along the route, which passed from the Gandhara region of the Indian subcontinent to the Taklamakan Desert, graffiti carved into stones have been discovered. Some of the stones have images of Siddhartha Gautama, also known as Gautama Buddha, and texts in two Indic scripts, Kharosthi and the later script of Brahmi.

Archaeological evidence from Niya and Loulan paint a complex picture of the cultural origins of the populations of the two cities. Some artifacts have stylistic characteristics that indicate their makers came from the Gandhara region (northwest Pakistan and northeast Afghanistan). Corpses disinterred at Niya and Loulan are not Chinese or Indian; they are instead Caucasoid with fair hair, light skin, and around six feet in height. This leads to speculation that the Niyans and Loulans were descendants of migrants from the Iranian Plateau. The textiles that wrapped these corpses, which date from the 2nd to 4th centuries CE, consist of cotton and silk. The former came from the west and the latter from the east.

Descriptions of the peoples of the region of the Taklamakan Desert exist in two ancient texts, *The History of the Han Dynasty* (82 CE) and the subsequent *History of the Later Han* (445 CE). The region is identified by the Chinese writers as the Kingdom of Shanshan. The two cities in the Kingdom of Shanshan, Niya and Loulan, seem to have vied with each other in importance when it came to the spread of Buddhism and the Indic Kharosthi language.

It was Zhang Qian's report that encouraged Emperor Wu to attack Loulan in 108 BCE. The king of Loulan was captured, and tribute was demanded by the Han emperor. Loulan, through alternating alliances between the Han and the Xiongnu, managed to stave off conquest. In 77 BCE, though, matters came to a head. After a series of Han envoys had been killed by the king of Loulan, Emperor Zhao (r. 87 BCE–74 BCE) sent an envoy named Fu Jiezi to Loulan. He delivered a gift of silk from China to the king of Loulan. The king, delighted with the gift, is said to have become intoxicated, and Fu's guard killed him. According to the Chinese records, Fu's assassin announced, "The Son of Heaven [the Han emperor] has sent me to punish the king, by reason of his crime in turning against Han...Han troops are about to arrive here; do not dare to make any move which would result in yourselves bringing about the destruction of your state." The Chinese then occupied the Kingdom of Loulan and attempted to annex it into the Han Empire under the designation Shanshan. The region, however, in periods when the Chinese showed signs of weakness, either reverted to being an independent kingdom or fell under the control of the Xiongnu. Han records say that in 25 CE, Loulan was allied with the Xiongnu. The Chinese responded by sending an army officer, Ban Chao, to force Loulan to return to Han control. When Ban Chao, along with a small contingent of soldiers, arrived in Loulan, he discovered a Xiongnu delegation negotiating with the king of Loulan. Ban killed the Xiongnu envoys and delivered their heads to King Guang, the ruler of Loulan, who then submitted to Han authority. This ensured that the first leg of the Silk Road from China toward the West was safe for traders and merchants.

Following the pacification of the peoples of the Shanshan Basin and forcing them to accede to Han control, Ban Chao decided to make contact with the far-away Roman Empire. He dispatched an ambassador, Gan Ying, to travel to the West. Exactly what Ban Chao knew about the Romans, whose empire at the time extended to Mesopotamia, is not known. Presumably, he acquired some knowledge of what lay beyond Persia from the traders in Loulan. Ambassador Gan Ying, whose goal was to reach the "western sea," may have reached the Mediterranean or Black Sea. However, it is more likely that he got only as far as the Persian Gulf. Learning that the journey across whatever sea he encountered involved a three-month roundtrip, he abandoned his expedition. His description of the Roman Empire, certainly based on second-hand observations, included information on the goods produced there, among them gold, silver, coins, jade, rhinoceros' horns, coral, amber, glass, and silk rugs with interwoven gold thread. It is clear from Gan Ying's mission that authorities and traders in Loulan believed that commerce and trading with the Han Chinese could be expanded by missions to the unknown West.

It has been suggested that Gan Ying's journey west was sabotaged by the Parthians, whose empire stretched from Mesopotamia, north to the Caspian Sea, and east into central Asia, almost to the frontiers of Chinese Shanshan. The Parthians, wishing to protect their role as the middlemen in the trade between Rome and India, as well as to advance their potential for trade farther east with China, may have discouraged Gan Ying by exaggerating the difficulties of the continuation of his expedition in a long sea crossing to the Roman Empire.

After Gan Ying's journey to the West, the Han emperor worked to cement their control of Shanshan and prevent subsequent kings of Loulan from harboring notions of independence. Soldiers were dispatched to Loulan, where they settled as colonists. By 222 CE, Shanshan had become a formal tributary of the Chinese. Affirmation of the inferior dependent status of Shanshan is indicated by the fact that the king was sent as a hostage to the Chinese court during the reign of the first emperor of the Jin dynasty, Emperor Wu (r. 266–290). The lengths to which the Chinese had to go through to deal with Shanshan indicates that the trade along the Silk Road was financially advantageous to the Han emperor.

In the *History of the Later Han,* which was compiled in the fifth century from earlier texts, it is recorded that the first ambassadors from the Romans arrived in the capital of the Han Empire during the reign of Emperor Huan (r. 146–168). It is not clear whether the emissaries were sent by Antoninus Pius (r. 138–161) or his successor Marcus Aurelius (r. 161–180). The Roman embassy arrived by sea, perhaps via the Gulf of Tonkin, which is located off the coast of northern Vietnam and southern China. This first group of Romans to visit the Han court became suspect because the gifts they presented were objects acquired in Southeast Asia rather than unique objects from Rome itself. It has been surmised by historians that the visitors to the Han court were, in fact, not a group of official ambassadors but rather merchants who had been shipwrecked and had thus lost the Roman goods they intended to deliver to the Chinese. The theory that the first contact between the Romans and the Chinese was through Southeast Asia is confirmed by other texts and archaeological finds involving mercantile connections between Rome and modern-day Cambodia and Vietnam. In 226 CE, a trader named in the texts as Qin Lun—a Chinese version of an unknown Roman name—appeared at the court of Emperor Sun Quan in Nanjing. After describing his Roman homeland, Qin Lun was dispatched back to the West. It is likely that Qin Lun, like earlier merchants, was a Roman trader who landed in Southeast Asia.

Chapter 4 – Buddhists along the Silk Road

The early history of what was to become known in the modern era as the Silk Road does not indicate that the silk trade was the primary goal in forging trade expansion in either the East or the West. The Greeks and Romans were primarily interested in expansion as they pushed into Asia Minor, and the Han Chinese were motivated to expand west in their goal of trading foodstuffs, horses, and a limited range of luxury goods with the settled and semi-nomadic peoples living there.

The towns and cities along the ancient trading routes, some of which were merely small oases and others sophisticated urban centers, were important not only for the exchange of goods but for the transmission of culture in all its forms, including language and religion.

In order to understand the spread of culture via the Silk Road, it is necessary to turn to the prosperous oasis city of Kucha. It was the gateway to the Chinese trade route that skirted the Taklamakan Desert to the north. Like Loulan, it became the nexus for the transmission of culture. The language of Kucha, Kuchean, came from the same Indo-European language group as Sanskrit, the original language for the expression of Buddhist teachings.

The Chinese first interacted with the peoples of Kucha in the late second century BCE. Han Emperor Wu sent his general Li Guangli to visit the kingdom of Fergana in modern-day Uzbekistan. On the way, he visited Kucha. Like in Loulan, the leaders of Kucha had attempted to appease the Xiongnu confederation, but as the Xiongnu weakened, the Kuchans became allied with the Han Chinese. In 65 BCE, the king of Kucha traveled to Chang'an, and after that, the Chinese had an official report on the oasis settlements along the northern route of the Silk Road around the Taklamakan Desert. The reports sent back by the officials in Kucha became incorporated into the official history of the Han dynasty.

The extent of the presence of the Hans in the region is difficult to assess. The oasis kingdoms along the northern route of what we call the Silk Road were continuously at war with one another. Thus, Kucha, in 46 BCE, was defeated by the neighboring oasis kingdom of Yarkand. The Han Chinese seem to have subsequently exerted control intermittently over various oases surrounding Kucha. General Ban Chao, who was named governor of the region in 91 CE, gained formal control of Kucha itself. His garrison at Kucha, which he placed under the control of the Bai family, lasted less than twenty years. Peoples of the region rose up against the Chinese rule and destroyed the Chinese garrison at Kucha. The Bai family, from time to time, succeeded over the centuries in gaining dominance over one oasis or another. They became Buddhists, and Buddhism became the dominant religion in Kucha by the 4th century.

It was in Kucha that Buddhist writings were translated from Sanskrit into Chinese by Kumarajiva (lived 344 to 413 CE). Kumarajiva was the son of a devout Buddhist mother who abandoned her husband and settled in a Buddhist nunnery. She traveled with her son to Gandhara, where Kumarajiva studied Hinayana Buddhism and then studied under a Mahayana Buddhist monk. He returned home to Kucha, bringing the two strands of Buddhism back to his people.

In 384 CE, the city of Kucha was conquered again, this time by the Chinese general Lü Chuang. Kucha was said to have had thousands of pagodas and temples, and the palace of the Bai kings was described as being equal to the residence of the gods. The holy Kumarajiva was kidnapped around 390 BCE, and according to his biography, he fathered children, which was against his Buddhist vows. Eventually, he arrived in the Chinese capital of the Jin dynasty (265–420 CE), Chang'an, in 401, where he was put in charge of translating Buddhist texts. Among the many texts he translated was the Lotus Sutra (a sutra is the Sanskrit word for a work said to be by Buddha himself). Kumarajiva's texts were widely circulated, and understanding them was eased by the Chinese invention of the pinyin system, in which certain characters were developed to represent syllables of foreign words. The expansion of the Chinese language so that certain Sanskrit words for Buddhist concepts could be understood may have involved the invention of as many as 35,000 new Chinese words.

The translation of Sanskrit texts in this period was not restricted to the Jin capital, Chang'an. In Kucha and elsewhere along the Silk Road, Buddhist texts were translated into local languages.

During the lifetime of Kumarajiva, work began on the now world-famous caves of Kizil, which are located 67 kilometers (almost 42 miles) west of Kucha. Discovered by a German explorer in 1909, the 339 excavated caves were decorated with paintings that have been used by art historians to unravel the cultural history of the region. The caves of Kizil consist of single rooms centered on a pillar, or stupa, around which Buddhists walked, expressing their devotion to Buddha. The construction of the caves is similar to those in India at Ajanta, near Bombay, and other early Buddhist caves in India. Some of the paintings, such as that of cave 38, show Indian gods and flaming Buddhas depicted in a distinctly Indian style. They were painted by artists from India or copied from drawings brought from India. Other caves are decorated with illustrations of Jataka tales, which are stories concerning Gautama Buddha's previous incarnations as both humans and animals. The tales, dating from 300 BCE to 400 CE, involved Buddha helping characters who found themselves in trouble. Since the discovery of the caves of Kizil, antiquarians from several nations have removed a lot of the artwork and deposited it in museums in the West.

The Bai family continued to rule in Kucha from the 6th through the 8th centuries. During this period, taxes were rendered to the reigning Chinese dynasties. Information on trade has been gleaned from Kuchan official passes for caravans that exist for the period of 641 to 644. Generally, the caravans were small, with less than ten men and a small number of animals, either donkeys or horses. Since the roads were safe, the caravans could consist of a small number of men who didn't require the protection of warriors. In 648, Tang Chinese (618-907) soldiers conquered Kucha again, wresting it from being a dependency of the Western Turkic Khaganate, which was formed at the beginning of the 7th century. Tang Chinese control over Kucha, the easternmost city along the northern Silk Road, was intermittently broken by revolts and incursions by Tibetans and Sogdians. The Tang Anxi Protectorate (647-784), established by the Tang military government, managed to hold onto control of Kucha, but contact with Chang'an along the Silk Road was occasionally broken. A Chinese general named Guo Xin held control of Kucha from 766. He ruled in isolation until 790 when the Tibetans from the south moved in. They, in turn, were displaced by the Uyghurs, who controlled the area from the early 9th century to the rise of the Mongol Empire in the 13th century.

Trade between China and the Kuchans throughout the 7th and 13th centuries was mainly restricted to horses. These were obtained from the nomadic tribes who grazed their herds north of Kucha and from the Sogdians to the west. The horses were exchanged for agricultural goods, steel, or cloth. There is also evidence that there was a monetized economy in the form of Chinese coins. When the Tang withdrew from Kucha in 755, a local currency was minted.

Chapter 5 – Turfan: An Oasis on the Silk Road

The second-most important oasis city on the Silk Road route to the north of the Taklamakan Desert was Turfan. The original inhabitants of the Turfan region were called Chü-shih by the Chinese, meaning people who lived in felt tents. By 60 BCE, the Han had pushed out the Xiongnu, a loose confederacy of nomadic tribes who lived in the eastern Eurasian Steppe, and controlled the land once occupied by the Chü-shih. The Han, for administrative purposes, split the newly subservient peoples into eight states, making the region around Turfan, the former Chü-shih kingdom, their center of operations. The garrison at Turfan included a military colony, and by 273 CE, the majority of the population of Turfan was primarily Chinese immigrants. The city changed hands regularly, but for the most part, it remained under Chinese control. With the collapse of the Western Qin dynasty in the 4th century CE, Turfan suffered from incursions by nomadic tribesmen. It was, after a concerted military effort, that the region around Turfan was restored to Chinese control under the Ch'ü family, who administered the territory from their capital at Kao-ch'ang some 40 kilometers (almost 25 miles) from modern-day Turfan.

Kao-ch'ang served as the administrative capital of the Turfan region under members of the Ch'ü family, who styled themselves as the kings of Liang. It was under Chü-ch'ü An-chou that an important Buddhist monastery was founded near Turfan. When it was explored by European archaeologists in the early 20th century, it revealed a treasure trove of information about the cultural history of the Turfan segment of the Silk Road.

In 460 CE, Chü-ch'ü An-chou was overthrown by a confederacy of nomadic tribes from the Gobi Desert, who then set up their own kingdom in Kao-ch'ang. In spite of the barbarian incursions, Turfan remained the base for administration under the Ch'ü family of kings (500–640) and subsequently under the Chinese administrators of the Tang dynasty (618–907) and finally the Uyghur Qocho kingdom (866–1283). By 981, there were more than fifty Buddhist temples in the vicinity of Turfan.

When the southern route around the Taklamakan Desert fell into disuse after 500 CE, travelers chose the northern route that passed through the city of Turfan. A description of the city exists in the writings of a Chinese monk named Xuanzang (c.602–664), who set out from Chang'an for India in 629. His purpose was to study Sanskrit Buddhist texts. From the westernmost city that was under the control of the Tang Chinese, Xuanzang proceeded west across the Gobi Desert and arrived in Turfan, which was about 650 kilometers (almost 404 miles) northeast of Kucha, in 630.

From Turfan, the Silk Road passed into Sogdia. After its invasion by the Muslims in the 8th century, the dominant religion, after a period of gradual conversion, became Islam.

Sogdia was a network of city-states where merchants traveled from one oasis to another, linking with Byzantium, India, Indochina, and China. Since its exploration by Zhang Qian during the reign of Han Emperor Wu in the 2nd century BCE, Sogdia was known to the Chinese as Kangju. Trade along the Silk Road between Sogdia and China, which had proceeded more or less unhindered in the Tang era, was interrupted by the collapse of the Tang Dynasty in 907 CE.

In the north and west of China, the Uyghur tribal confederacy broke up in the mid-10th century. The Uyghurs, a Turkic ethnic group that migrated from Mongolia into the region north of the Taklamakan Desert in the 9th century, converted to Islam in the 10th century. With multi-ethnic conflicts rife along the north and south Silk Road routes around the Taklamakan Desert, there was an interruption in long-distance trade.

Although these kinds of disturbances along the Silk Road interrupted trade, the rise of a people called the Khitans might have interrupted it worse. The Khitans were a nomadic people who moved with the seasons over grazing lands in modern-day Mongolia, Russian Far East, and parts of China. They were, according to scholars, proto-Mongolians who spoke Khitan.

A leader of the Yila tribe of the Khitans, by the name of Abaoji, set out in the first quarter of the 10th century to unify the Khitans and conquer neighboring peoples. Leading a 70, 000-man cavalry, he rode into Shanxi (a modern-day province of northern China), where he made an alliance with the military governor, Li Keyong, who in 833 had unified and pacified Shanxi under the authority of the Tang Dynasty. From the capital of Chang'an, the emperors of the Tang Dynasty created a highly cultured civilization—according to some, it was the golden age of China—and through force, they pacified nomadic tribes to the west along the Silk Road. These tribes of Inner Asia were put under a protectorate system and required to pay tribute to China.

With his successes in taking Tang Chinese territories in northern China, Abaoji assumed the title of Khagan of the Khitans. Later known after his death as Emperor Taizu of Liao (r. 916–926), he attempted to organize his people under an administration that combined the traditions of nomadic society and the Chinese system of government that had been adopted by the sedentary peoples he annexed into his empire. For instance, in Abaoji's court, Chinese formalities were observed. He went so far as to call himself Celestial Emperor in the Chinese style. In contradiction to Khitan tradition, in which leadership was won by merit, he named his son as the heir apparent. By the time of his death, Abaoji had conquered all of the tribes to the east in the Korean Peninsula, the Russian Far East, and Manchuria. Also, he had spread his authority well into the Mongolian Plateau. However, Abaoji did not live to follow his ambition to move south to attack the Tang Chinese. After an internecine struggle, Taizong became the second emperor of Liao (r. 927–947). He succeeded where his father had failed—he marched into China, proceeded to cross the Yellow River, and threatened to move west to Chang'an. Rebellions and treachery among his own forces and the Chinese rebel families he conquered forced Taizong to retreat and return beyond the Yellow River. When he died, his successor could not keep the territorial gains. The Liao dynasty faded in importance until it fell to the Northern Song dynasty of China in 1125.

Further disruptions in the trade along the Silk Road were caused by warfare in the north between the Song Chinese and the rival Great Jin dynasty (1115–1234). The conflict forced the Song armies and court to retreat to the south, giving up control of a vast swath of northern China, principally Manchuria, to the Jurchen rebels, who were at first allies of the Jin and later became their overlords.

Following their retreat to the south, trade for the Song Chinese came to be less reliant on the Silk Road, as it had become increasingly dangerous and unreliable. Commerce along the Silk Road was, in part, supplanted by maritime trade with Japan, Southeast Asia, and around the Indian Ocean. Chinese ports along the southern coast, such as Guangzhou and Quanzhou, became important trading centers with Arab, Persian, Malay, and Tamil traders who carried out their business there.

Chapter 6 – The Legend of Prester John

In the early Middle Ages, Europeans had only the sketchiest of ideas of what laid east beyond Mesopotamia. Legends of Alexander's conquests in the East were passed down in oral literature and eventually put into writing. These were, for the most part, fanciful tales that referred to strange creatures such as Amazons, Cynocephali (dog-headed men), Sciopods (one-legged men who were swift runners), and Anthropophagi (men with faces on their chests). Strange beasts were also said to inhabit the East, like unicorns and serpents with two feet.

European interest in the lands that lay in the East beyond the Mediterranean was stimulated by the fervor for crusading against the Muslims. The Muslims had expanded their sphere of influence well beyond the Holy Land when the First Crusade was launched in 1096. The initiation of trade with the unknown Eastern lands was of less importance than spreading the Christian religion to counter Muslim expansionism in the East.

In the 12th century, the legends of the East were expanded with the inclusion of the tale of Prester John. In 1122, a man claiming to be the patriarch of India arrived in Rome, demanding papal confirmation of his office. Contemporary texts exist which purported to record Prester John's description of India as he presented it to Pope Callixtus II. Prester John, it was said, told the pope that he lived in the huge city of Hulna, which was inhabited by devout Christians and surrounded by twelve monasteries. The tale of a vibrant Christian community beyond the Tigris River was reiterated by the German chronicler Bishop Otto of Freising. He wrote in 1145 that he had heard from a Syrian bishop that a king and priest named John ruled over a vast kingdom of Nestorian Christians descended from the Magi, which many readers may be familiar with their depiction in the story of the birth of Jesus as the three men who traveled from the East to pay homage to the infant Christ. Otto of Freising reported that the eastern king John would have come to the aid of the besieged Christian Crusaders in the Near East had he not been prevented from doing so by the impossibility of ferrying his army across the Tigris.

The legend of Prester John was further expanded in an anonymously authored *Letter of Prester John*, which was created sometime before 1180 and addressed to Byzantine Emperor Manuel I Comnenus (r. 1143–1180). The letter became a very popular document, and there are more than 120 manuscript copies of it.

In the letter, Prester John says that he wishes to travel to the West and visit the Sepulcher of Christ. He says that he rules over a vast kingdom with 62 Christian sub-kings and that his realm is extraordinarily prosperous, flowing with milk and honey. It is adjacent to Paradise, has a fountain of youth, and there is no venial sin in his land. Prester John reports that he has an enormous army with knights and crossbowmen. In summary, he concludes, "There is no king as powerful in this world as am I."

The manuscript copies of the letter varied, and the description of Prester John's kingdom was expanded. For instance, in the copies created in England, it was said that in the eastern court of Prester John, there were some 11,000 Englishmen. In France, the copies of the letter claimed that Prester John had 11,000 French knights in his command.

The popularity of the *Letter of Prester John* suggests that there was a widespread hope in Europe during the Middle Ages that a powerful Christian community in the East could assist in the Crusaders' struggle against the Muslim "infidels." Besides that, the fact that there was a spectacular kingdom somewhere in the uncharted territory of the East supplied a kind of hope for a better world among the Europeans.

The Arab geographers in the courts of the Muslim enemies of the Crusaders had equally fanciful notions about what lay to the east of their expanding caliphates. From tales related by seaborne traders who penetrated the East, Muslim scholars concocted confusing reports of India, the East Indies, and China. By the early 14th century, a Kurdish geographer named Abu al-Fida (1273–1331) stated that knowledge of China was "as good as unknown to us; there being few travellers who arrive from these parts, such as might furnish us with intelligence." What little information that was conveyed in the Arab geographical texts relating to the East was not adopted by the Europeans, who, for some reason, ignored the Arab geographical texts, despite having an enthusiastic interest in the scientific writings of the Muslims.

The Europeans were knowledgeable about Christians in the far reaches of the Levant, though. They were adherents to a doctrine condemned by the Christians of the Eastern Rite in Constantinople and the Roman Catholic Church. The Nestorians held the heretical view that in Christ there was but one person with two natures, divine and human. The head of the Nestorian Church was in Baghdad, and their churches were spread throughout the Near East from Syria to Persia. The Nestorians were active proselytizers, and by the 8th century, Nestorian churches could be found in Turkestan, China, and among the nomadic tribes in Mongolia.

The Nestorian Christians came into contact with the Chinese in the 12th century. A breakaway Chinese king, Yelü Dashi, led a group of nomadic Khitan clans into central Asia, where he set himself up as the emperor of Qara Khitai, also known as Western Liao. He established a central authority over a vast region encompassing trade routes around Lake Balkhash. He set up his capital at Balasagun in modern-day Kyrgyzstan. To the west of Qara Khitai, in what is now Iran and Iraq, the Seljuk Sultanate held sway. The enormous armies of Yelü Dashi and the Seljuks met on the battlefield at Qatwan, located north of Samarkand in modern-day Uzbekistan, in 1141. Yelü Dashi's forces prevailed, and he moved on to Samarkand, where he accepted the allegiance of the Muslim leaders there and established a tribute state. It was Yelü Dashi's tolerance of Nestorian Christians in his empire that no doubt became the basis for the legend of Prester John, which proliferated in Europe after the First Crusade (1095–1099).

Chapter 7 – Genghis Khan, Ruler of the Whole World

In the 10th century, the proto-Mongol tribes living in the region of the upper reaches of the Amur River began to leave their ancestral lands in what is today Inner Mongolia and Manchuria. They moved south and west, invading the northern reaches of China, where they founded the Liao dynasty (916-1125). Under the name of the Qara Khitai, they established themselves as sedentary farmers, established a capital city named Huangdu (later Shangjing), and adopted a system of hereditary leadership, abandoning their traditional tribal system of electing a leader. Situated along the Silk Road, the peoples of the Khitan federation had ready access to the ununified states of China. It was along the Silk Road that elements of Chinese culture traveled, such as the idea that stabilization of taxes was advantageous to the growth of wealth. Around 920, the first ruler of the Liao dynasty, Abaoji (r. 916-926), adopted the Chinese name of Taizu. With a need for written documents to facilitate the administration of the Khitan people, the Liao emperor had his court scholars adapt a script from written documents that came into the empire from Chinese traders along the Silk Road. With the knowledge of Chinese culture that traveled north with traders, the

Liao emperors were inspired to invade the richer and more sophisticated Chinese.

In 960, fifty years after the collapse of the Tang dynasty in China, the country was unified under the Song dynasty (969–1279). The Song ruled a much smaller swath of China than the Tang. The third Song emperor, Zhenzong (r. 968–1022), negotiated a treaty with Liao to the north, promising to annually deliver a tribute of 200,000 bolts of silk as well as a vast amount of silver. This treasure passed along one of the routes of the Silk Road, as did other goods in the period of peace between the Liao and the Song. Paying a tribute in silk was traditional with the Chinese, and it became a means of exchange that was ubiquitous on the Silk Road in regions adjacent to China. The bolts of silk turned over to the Liao could be used as payment for foodstuffs and horses raised by sedentary farmers and nomadic herdsmen. In turn, the merchants outside and within Liao territory could use the bolts of silk as currency to acquire other goods they required.

There was a gradual coalescing of nomadic Mongol tribes north of the Liao lands, who also assimilated with other tribes who ranged over the central Asian steppes. In 1155, a boy named Temüjin was born into a Mongol clan. He acquired unusual abilities as a warrior, and Temüjin eventually acquired control of all of Mongolia. His demonstrated ability as a warrior and a statesman placed him in good stead when a *kurultai*, or Mongol political and military council, met in 1206 to consider his worthiness as a leader. Temüjin, better known as Genghis Khan, was appointed as the great khan of the Mongols. From this point on, he extended his power to form the greatest empire the world had ever seen. The many cultures that came to be dominated by the Mongols delivered tribute and traded amongst themselves using the Silk Road. With Mongol control, the trade routes became safer, and traveling with merchandise from west to east and vice versa became less complicated when the Mongols instituted common regulations for passes to travel along segments of the Silk Road.

Genghis Khan subdued the forest people to the north in Siberia, and he attacked the people of the Gobi Desert, then forming a full third of China. He also conquered the Karluks, a confederacy of nomadic Turkic peoples west of the Altai Mountains in central Asia, and subdued the closely allied Muslim Uyghurs, who occupied several oases across the Taklamakan Desert, thus controlling the Silk Road. He took the Khitans into his empire and then set out to conquer China itself. In March of 1211, Genghis Khan declared war on the remnants of the Jin in northern China, which was then under the control of the Jurchens. The going was slow, taking up to two years, during which Genghis Khan took the opportunity to conquer the Jurchens in Manchuria. In 1215, he took Beijing. He immediately returned to Mongolia and dealt with a rebellion in Qara Khitai, where he was received with enthusiasm by Muslims who believed themselves to be oppressed by the Buddhists.

By this time, the Mongols were in control of all of central Asia up to the river Syr Darya, which formed the border with Iran. With respect to the Silk Road, this Mongol suzerainty was an important impetus to the increase in traffic and trade. Iran, then under the control of Ala ad-Din Muhammad II (r. 1200–1220), the shah of the Khwarezmian dynasty, was attacked by Genghis Khan, who led between 150,000 and 200,000 soldiers as he marched toward the west. In September of 1219, Genghis crossed the Syr Darya and penetrated Khwarezmia as far as Bukhara (in modern-day Uzbekistan), then chased down Ala ad-Din Muhammad as he fled south into Bactra (present-day Balkh) and then to Nishapur and Rey (present-day Tehran). Genghis Khan leveled the country and killed many inhabitants; however, he spared the artisans and the Muslim clergy. The latter escaped retribution because Genghis Khan had a policy of protecting all religions and permitting all religious practices within his empire. The son of Ala ad-Din Muhammad, Jalal ad-Din Mingburnu (r. 1220–1231), kept up with the war, retreating into Sogdiana (present-day states of Samarkand

and Bokhara in Uzbekistan, Sughd in Tajikistan, and parts of Afghanistan). Genghis Khan's army pursued his enemy into Sogdiana, where his soldiers carried out ethnic cleansing on a grand scale. Jalal was forced to retreat across the Indus River, where he attempted to rebuild the Khwarezmian Empire. Genghis Khan did not immediately press on in pursuit of Jalal, but in 1222, he besieged Multan (in modern-day Pakistan). The Mongols were forced to withdraw, though, on account of the heat, and Genghis Khan then returned to the seat of his empire in Mongolia.

Due to the conquests in the west by Genghis Khan, the complex and inconsistent trading regulations and the interruption of trade due to local conflicts were slowly ameliorated. With the Mongols in charge, traders could move greater distances before off-loading their goods and handing them over to traders familiar with the local routes of the Silk Road. With the rise of the Mongols, trade along the routes of the Silk Road expanded, both in distance traveled as well as in the volume of goods moved. As the Mongol Empire expanded, so did the length of some of the routes of the Silk Road.

Rather than taking the most direct route home, Genghis Khan's army crossed the Caucasus Mountains, where they encountered the Georgians. The Georgians set up defensive positions in Ukraine, which was then under the control of the Kipchak Turks. The Russians were summoned to help in the battle against the Mongols but were roundly defeated on May 31ˢᵗ, 1222, by allies of Genghis Khan. Mongol Georgia was to become an important starting point for European traders to connect with the northern route along the silk road.

By 1222, the elderly Genghis Khan was facing his own mortality. He had heard that Chinese Taoists were in possession of a secret remedy against death, and so, he summoned a Taoist master to his traveling court, who told him that there were remedies to prolong life but not to avoid death. He advised temperance and good living. The Great Khan listened and then set out for Mongolia, arriving in 1225. Although weary of war, Genghis Khan personally led his army across the Gobi Desert and attacked the Tangut people in northwest China. It was during this time that Genghis Khan pushed to attack the people of the Western Xia, which are now known as the Chinese provinces of Ningxia, Gansu, Qinghai, Shaanxi, Xinjiang, and parts of Inner and Outer Mongolia. However, it would be his last season of fighting, as Genghis Khan died in 1227 before the Tanguts capitulated. However, the Western Xia, where the Silk Road ran from northern China to central Asia, finally fell under the control of the Mongols. With the Mongols dominating such a large area, encompassing China to the doorstep of Europe in Georgia and Ukraine, trading along the Silk Road became safe and profitable once again.

Because a successor to Genghis Khan could only be elected from his bloodline by a *kurultai*, the assembling of potential candidates took time since they had to be summoned from the far reaches of the Mongol Empire. Finally, Ögedei, Genghis's third son, was appointed as the next great khan, ruling from 1229 to 1241. Among his courtiers were warriors from his family who distinguished themselves with strings of victories that greatly expanded the empire as well as trade. Korea was conquered in 1236, thus pushing the Silk Road farther east. Ögedei Khan's successors as great khan annexed Tibet around 1250. This resulted in an increased movement of goods and ideas from Tibet, which moved along a Silk Road route that went north and east into China.

The Mongols renewed attacks on the Song Chinese emperors, who managed to hold off the Mongol armies from 1234 to 1279. In the west in 1236, the Mongols under the leadership of Ögedei Khan forced the Christian Georgians to become vassals of the Mongol state. This allowed for the extension of a safe Silk Road route up to the frontier with Christian Europe. The Armenians had also fallen under the sway of the Mongols as allies in their struggle to resist the imposition of Islam on their state. In 1254, Hethum I, the king of Armenia (r. 1226-1270), submitted his kingdom to Mongol suzerainty. To confirm this, he sent his brother Sempad to

Karakorum in 1247, which was the Mongol capital from 1235 to 1260. (Karakorum was in what today is the Övörkhangai Province of Mongolia near the modern town of Kharkhorin.) Sempad did not travel east along the Silk Road but rather went by sea to the court of the Mongol Empire. The arrangement between Armenia and Ögedei Khan was ratified in 1254 when King Hethum traveled overland across Asia along the Silk Road to meet the great khan. His trip was recorded in a text, *The Journey of Haithon, King of Little Armenia, To Mongolia and Back*, by the Armenian court historian Kirakos Gandzaketsi (c. 1200–1271). The story of the journey became popular in Europe and Russia, where there was a great interest in the Mongol Empire, the court of the great khan, and the trade along the overland routes from the exotic Eastern cultures. Among those most particularly drawn to the account were traders and merchants, who looked to get as much information on the Silk Road before engaging in what they believed would be profitable ventures to the seat of power of the mighty Mongol Empire.

The northwestern region of the Mongol Empire split from the control of the Mongol court in Karakorum in 1259. It became a separate khanate known as the Kipchak Khanate or the Ulus of Jochi. The latter name was applied because the region of the Mongol Empire, including southern Russia and Kazakhstan, had been given by Genghis Khan to his eldest son Jochi. When Jochi died, the area came under the control of his son, Batu Khan. In 1235, Batu led his army westward, capturing Volga Bulgaria, a state at the confluence of the Volga and Kama Rivers, in 1236 and part of the Ukrainian steppe in 1237. The Crimean Peninsula was conquered by the Mongols in 1238. Batu then moved north into Kievan Rus' and invaded Poland and Hungary and laid siege to Vienna.

As he realized he was facing a stronger foe, Batu retreated from Vienna. While doing so, he placed Bulgaria under Mongol control. It was under the reign of Batu Khan (r. 1227–1255) that the Mongol

Empire, which was at the doorstep of Europe and Russia, became known as the Golden Horde. This name first appeared in Russian texts dating from the middle of the 16th century; however, the origins of the designation remain shrouded in mystery. It is suspected that the word "horde" was derived from the Mongolic word *ordu*, meaning camp or headquarters. The appellation "golden" may have been derived from the golden tent used by Batu Khan.

With the Mongol Empire so close to the heart of European commerce, it is understandable that merchants in the newly rising city-states of Italy, as well as the various dukedoms and kingdoms in other regions of Europe, would begin to cast their eyes to the East in search of profits. This expansion of trade with the East along the continually lengthening Silk Road was even used by the Catholic Church, as clerics piggybacked on trading missions as a means of increasing papal authority through missionary work.

The imminent danger to Europe posed by the Golden Horde and indeed all of the Mongols, who were known collectively as the Tartars in the West, was remarked upon by Pope Alexander IV (pontiff from 1254 to 1261). His proclamation to what was referred to as "civilized nations" was intended to raise awareness of the threat from the East. He wrote, "There rings in the ears of all...a terrible trumpet of dire forewarning which...[of] the scourge of Heaven's wrath in the hands of the inhuman Tartars, erupting as it were from the secret confines of Hell." This kind of scaremongering had little effect on Christian merchants driven by cupidity rather than religious purity.

The expansion of the Golden Horde by Batu Khan, in effect, paved the way for Europeans to travel the full extent of the Silk Road through territories under the control of a single authority. The Mongol Empire, which extended from Europe to China, facilitated travel and trade through an assortment of minor kingdoms and cultures that, in the past, had hindered free passage for commerce. All of the different tribal, ethnic, and political entities along the Silk

Road, which were now under tight Mongol control, offered safe passage for travelers and merchants.

In Europe, the rise of the Mongols, or Tartars as they were known there, was noted by church leaders. A Dominican friar from Hungary on a journey into Mongol-held Russia in 1235 reported that the Mongols were about to conquer Rome and thus claim world domination and consequently destroy the Christian Church. According to Europeans at the time, the Mongols were beasts of the vilest character who were bent on a number of plots to upset the Near East and Europe itself. Pope Gregory IX (pontiff from 1227 to 1241) tried and failed to organize a Crusade against the Mongols. In March 1245, Pope Innocent IV (pontiff from 1243 to 1254) wrote letters to the "King and peoples of the Tartars," explaining Christian doctrine and asking for an explanation of the Mongol attacks against Christian peoples. These were to be presented by two groups of friars. One party was to travel to the Near East along the Silk Road to seek out the leaders of the Mongol forces, while another party was to travel through Poland and Russia to deliver the messages to the leader of the Mongols in Asia.

After passing through the Holy Land, the Dominican Friar, André de Longjumeau, arrived at Tabriz (in northwestern Iran). He delivered the pope's missives to Baycu Noyan, the leader of the Mongol forces in Armenia and Persia. Along the northern route to the Mongol headquarters, the Dominican Ascelin of Cremona, as the head of the papal delegation, traveled to Baycu's summer camp in the Armenian highlands in 1245. There he had the pope's letters translated into Persian and ensured that they were sent off to the court of the great khan at Karakorum in central Asia.

A third embassy was also sent to the Mongols. This one was led by the Franciscan friar Giovanni da Pian del Carpine. Setting out from Lyon in 1245, the ambassadors were joined by a Polish Franciscan, Brother Benedict, who would be able to act as a translator when the group passed through Slavic-speaking lands. They met Batu Khan and delivered letters from the pope. He convinced them that they needed to proceed to the court of the new great khan, Güyük (r. 1246-1248), who was the grandson of Genghis Khan. Their journey along the Silk Road took them through the former Khwarezmian Empire, where they saw "many devastated cities, destroyed castles, deserted villages," and through Qara Khitai, where they suffered from the intense cold. They eventually reached Güyük's camp near Karakorum in 1246.

At the camp, the Franciscans witnessed the ceremonies surrounding the enthronement of Güyük, the new great khan. Friar Giovanni da Pian del Carpine recorded that it was his observation that the great khan was a very intelligent man. He also noted that the Christians (Nestorians) who served in his household were of the belief that he would soon convert to Christianity. In spite of this, Güyük's reply to Pope Innocent IV was an uncompromising rebuttal of the pope's position. Güyük wrote that he rejected the pope's demand that the Mongols become Christian and assent to the superior power of the papacy.

> How dost thou know whom God forgives, to whom he shows mercy? By the power of God from the going up of the sun to his going down He had delivered all the lands to Us...Now you say with a sincere heart: 'We shall become your subject...' Thou in person, at the head of the kings, must all together at once come to do homage to Us. We shall then recognize your submission.

The pope's embassy returned along the Silk Road via Kiev, which they reached on June 9th, 1247. Over the course of their journey, Friar Giovanni and his party had covered some 6,000 kilometers (around 3,730 miles). While the envoys of Pope Innocent IV may have been unsuccessful in convincing the great khan of the supremacy of the Christian Church in Rome, Friar Giovanni, in his account of his journey, *Ystoria Mongalorum*, wrote very useful descriptions of the lands his mission passed through. The *Ystoria Mongalorum* is the first European chronicle of Mongol history, and it was chronicles like this that helped to motivate

European traders to seek the fortunes offered by commerce with the East.

The introduction to Giovanni's text reveals what became, for Europeans, the beginnings of knowledge about the Mongols, who were posing a severe threat to the Christian world. Giovanni wrote, "Wishing to write an account of the Tartars in which readers will be able to find their way about, we will divide it into chapters." These chapters deal with descriptions of the country of the Mongols and the peoples and religions of the Mongol Empire. In the final chapter, Giovanni discussed "how war should be waged against them." The detail of Giovanni's account is significant. Under the rubric of Mongol methods of warfare, he describes the organization of their army, weapons, armor, and siege tactics. His anthropological observations included, among other things, marriage customs, food, clothes, and burial practices. With respect to the geography of the Mongol Empire, Giovanni only discusses what he observed on his journey to and from Karakorum. The information Giovanni had gleaned on his trip was circulated through lectures he gave to his fellow Franciscans.

The next recorded contact between the Mongols and the Europeans occurred in December 1248 when two Nestorian Christians from within the Mongol Empire arrived in Cyprus, where King Louis IX of France (r. 1226–1270) was preparing for his Crusade against the Muslims in Egypt. The emissaries falsely said that the Mongol general Eljihidey, who commanded troops in Persia, and the Great Khan Güyük had converted to Christianity. The ambassadors also claimed that Güyük's mother was the daughter of Prester John, someone the Europeans knew well from popular legends. All of this was good news for the Crusaders under King Louis, and they sought to affirm the assistance of the Mongols in their fight against the Muslims. André de Longjumeau, already having made contact with the Mongols, was dispatched to Tabriz with appropriate gifts, but on his arrival, he learned that the Great Khan Güyük had died. The Mongol general Eljihidey sent the ambassadors to Karakorum, where the regent, Sorghaghtani Beki, in the midst of arranging for her son to ascend to the Mongol imperial throne, understood the gifts offered by the ambassadors to be a symbol of France's and Latin Europe's submission to the soon-to-be great khan. Sorghaghtani Beki then sent a letter to Louis IX, demanding that he appear at her court and deliver up appropriate tribute.

However, Louis, preoccupied with other matters, abandoned his attempted alliance with the Mongols. A Franciscan in his entourage, William of Rubruck, convinced the French king to permit him to travel as a missionary to see Batu and convince him that the Mongols of the Golden Horde should convert to Christianity. William and a companion, Friar Bartolomeo of Cremona, set off from Cyprus in May of 1253. They passed through Constantinople and sailed across the Black Sea to the Crimean Peninsula. They then rode on horseback, accompanied by a wagon train, to the camp of Sartaq Khan, the son and eventual successor to Batu Khan. Sartaq sent them on to Batu's camp beyond the Volga, and Batu, in turn, sent the friars on to the court of the new Great Khan Möngke (r. 1251-1259) at Karakorum. There, they were allowed to stay for six months. However, William of Rubruck and his companion were unsuccessful in their missionary goals.

In his account of the Mongols, William of Rubruck describes many details of life in the capital, mentioning the use of Chinese paper money, the scribes who wrote in Chinese characters, and the appearance and practices of Buddhist monks. William also notes the presence of Europeans in the Mongol capital, among whom was a Parisian goldsmith who had made a silver tree and four silver lions for the palace of the great khan. According to William, there were twelve pagan temples, two mosques, and a Nestorian church in the capital, the latter which was used by the Hungarians, Russians, Georgians, and Armenians in the community, as well as some of the khan's own family. William was unsuccessful in reaching his goal, the conversion of the great khan. He reported that the Great Khan

Möngke had told William of his belief in the last conversation they had together. "As God has given different fingers to the hand, so he has given different ways to men." William left behind his companion Friar Bartolomeo and departed Karakorum with little to show for his missionary zeal. He arrived at Batu's camp in 1254, crossed the Caucasus Mountains, and entered the Holy Land. From there, he sent his report to Louis IX, who was then back in France. His Crusade in Egypt had ended with his capture by the Muslims in 1250. After being ransomed, he had spent four years in the Holy Land before returning to France.

William's descriptions of his travels to Karakorum and back are much more detailed than that of his predecessors. He wrote in great detail about the geography of the Mongol Empire as he traveled along the Silk Road. He also described the cultures and customs of the lands he passed through and characterized the conditions in Mongol military camps as appalling. "I can't find the words to tell you of the misery we suffered when we came to the encampments." The wretched conditions, wrote William, indicated that the Mongols would be no threat if the pope were to declare a Crusade against them.

Around the middle of the 13th century, information on the Mongol Empire was, despite the records of emissaries to the East, often incorrect or scant, and what little there was of it was not widely diffused. It is known that the fourth great khan, Möngke, renewed Mongol expansion. With his brother Kublai, he began to push into China. In the west, his younger brother Hülegü (ruler of the Ilkhanate from 1256 to 1265) invaded Iraq and took over the power of the Abbasid Caliphate. Hülegü moved into Syria and then conquered Aleppo and Damascus in 1260, receiving the vassalage of the Christian nobles in those cities. He was forced to retreat back to Azerbaijan upon hearing the news of the death of his brother, the great khan. The forces Hülegü left behind were defeated by the Mamluk sultan of Egypt, Saif ad-Din Qutuz, in the Battle of Ain

Jalut near Galilee on September 3rd, 1260. It was this battle that ended the belief in the West that the Mongols were invincible.

While all of this was going on, the Silk Road had been traveled by a number of Europeans, almost exclusively emissaries of the Christian Church, who left records of their journeys. It is known that the journey to the East was accomplished by many others as well, primarily merchants, who did not leave records. The fact that European traders are mentioned in the accounts as being present in the East is not surprising, as for some time, under the auspices of the Mongol Empire, the Silk Road had evolved into something that resembles a modern highway—albeit with less traffic, of course.

It was in the last half of the 13th century that one of medieval Europe's most dazzling travelers left a record of his journey. Many readers will be familiar with the name of Marco Polo, who journeyed to the East along the Silk Road to visit the fabled court of the great khan. His host and employer in the East was none other than the warrior Kublai Khan, who expanded the Mongol Empire, lost the first major battles beyond the Mongol frontiers, and was the founder of a Chinese dynasty of emperors.

Chapter 8 – The Lord of Xanadu, Kublai Khan: The Emperor of China

The ascension to the throne of great khan by Genghis Khan's grandson, Kublai, who was in his forties, in 1260 marked the beginning of a new era in Mongol history. Not only did the Mongol Empire expand and become a highly organized imperial state, but it also reached a peak of sophistication before the empire began to crumble. It was the era when the land route from the West to the East along the Silk Road saw its highest level of activity before gradually being replaced by seaborne trade.

Kublai, who was born in 1215, was brought up under the tutelage of a Buddhist nursemaid. In his youth, he became enamored with Chinese culture. Because he was a minor princeling, just one among many in the extended family of descendants of Genghis Khan, he was not expected to have an important role. Kublai, in his youth, is mentioned here and there in the chronicles of his uncles and grandfather, *The Secret History of the Mongols*, which was written after the death of Genghis Khan. What little is recorded about

Kublai's youth is thanks to the widespread importance of his mother, Sorghaghtani Beki.

In order to pacify the rebellious Kerait steppe people, Genghis Khan arranged for his youngest son, Tolui, to marry Sorghaghtani, the daughter of the leader of the insurrectionist Kerait. This marriage alliance produced four sons, among whom was Kublai. Sorghaghtani, after the death of her husband, assumed power and promoted the religion of her family, Nestorian Christianity. Some in the West believed that it was her uncle who was the fabled Christian King Prester John. Whether Sorghaghtani's uncle was a Christian or not, it is unlikely that he would have traveled to the west with an army to assist the Crusaders.

Kublai Khan's ascent to the throne of the Mongol Empire was not simple. The matter of succession after Genghis Khan died was as one would expect in a newly formed empire—complicated. The great khan's Genghis's eldest son, Jochi, who seemed the most likely successor, predeceased his father, and his sons made no effort to assume power. Before dying, Genghis Khan had decreed that his third son, Ögedei, would succeed him if he was worthy. When Genghis died, his sons and grandsons fought to determine who was worthy of taking on the leadership of the Mongol Empire. Ögedei prevailed at a *kurultai*, or council meeting, and set about changing the administration in the Mongol Empire. In turning the more or less chaotic administration into something more civilized, Ögedei instituted a mounted postal system, built granaries, and instituted property taxes. The postal system, which worked through a kind of "pony express," required the construction of roads along which mounted couriers could cover as many as 250 miles a day. These roads also served to facilitate the transport of goods from one region to another.

Great Khan Ögedei, with the help of his family, including Kublai, attempted to stabilize territories outside Mongolia itself. By doing this, they ensured that the Mongols were sustained financially, thus alleviating the need for constant pillage of frontier lands in order to provide sufficient food for their people.

Ögedei further developed a spot marked out by his grandfather as a suitable Mongol capital, which Genghis Khan had named Karakorum or "Black Rock." It was there that Ögedei set up a town with four walls of rammed earth and an inner palace for the Mongol royals. Karakorum never did become a major city, but its adjacency to the Buddhist Erdene Zuu Monastery and its situation in the Orkhon Valley, which allowed them to be close to the Xiongnu and Uyghur peoples, permitted the establishment of a new centralized authority for the Mongol Empire. Mongol warlords set up encampments around the city, and Ögedei himself is said to have pulled up his portable palace there when he was not at war elsewhere. It was apparently a wagon ten meters (almost 33 feet) wide, drawn by 22 oxen.

From Karakorum, the Mongols controlled northern China through a kind of prime minister, a Chinese man named Yelü Chucai. The success of Yelü Chucai's management of China is indicated by the fact that he turned over around one thousand silver ingots of tax income in 1230. The importance of Karakorum in Mongol life, in spite of it being the capital, was minimal. According to Mongol custom, it was the duty of the youngest son of a warrior to remain at home and manage family affairs, primarily grazing the family livestock on what became overgrazed land. Elder sons were expected to go to war, pillage enemies, deal with revolts, and generally work to expand Mongol control everywhere. Ögedei, thus free from holding court in Karakorum, was at liberty to lead an army to attack northern Korea, which had stubbornly held off Mongol rule. Ögedei also dispatched an army to Iran to deal with the remaining Seljuk Turks there, and he led an army himself in regular incursions against China. A heavy drinker like most Mongols, Ögedei was stricken with a palsy, perhaps a stroke, that was brought on by intemperance. He was treated by shamans, who required the transference of the affliction to Tolui, Ögedei's younger brother. It is likely that the treatment involved the consumption of vast quantities of alcohol by Tolui, who died in the process in 1232. Ögedei, who was severely debilitated, continued to rule for another twenty years.

During those twenty years, Sorghaghtani, Tolui's wife, refused to remarry, which was the custom among the Mongols. She became the most powerful Mongol woman, having been bequeathed considerable land by her husband, which meant that she was both wealthy and powerful. Sorghaghtani's son, Kublai, was raised in a different environment than most Mongol warriors. Instead of following his father off to war, he led a sedentary life practicing hunting and the arts of war in the steppes around Karakorum. He was supplied with a Uyghur tutor from central Asia and learned how to read the Turkic script used by the Mongols.

Sorghaghtani, at some point, moved her family and court to the Hebei province in China. This was a territory that was rightfully hers since it had been conquered by her late husband. Hebei, however, was in ruins not only from the Mongol invasion but also because many of its residents had fled south into Song China to escape Mongol rule. More Chinese were forced to exit Hebei when the Mongols instituted punishing taxes on them. It is thought that the region, once home to forty million people, had been reduced to having around ten million inhabitants. Sorghaghtani's rule of Hebei was much more humane than the average Mongol control over other peoples. Sorghaghtani, as a Nestorian Christian, was tolerant and funded the establishments of other religions. Her administration also encouraged Chinese farmers to continue tilling the land. The conditions there were so amenable that some Chinese returned from the Song Empire in the south. By facilitating farming, Sorghaghtani was going against the Mongol custom of turning over captured farmland to nomadic herdsmen, who turned the once productive farms into pastures. In 1240, when her son Kublai was in his twenties, Sorghaghtani gave him the region of Jingzhou in southern Hubei on the banks of the Yangtze River. At first, Kublai neglected his estate, and it fell into ruin. Its tax income was stolen by agents of the Mongols and thus was not rendered to Kublai as it should have been. In an effort at reform, Kublai took a page from his mother's book of administration and regularized the management of his estate through Chinese agents, who were charged with reducing taxes and encouraging farming. The population of Jingzhou increased as the refugees returned to their lands.

When in 1241 Ögedei Khan finally drank himself to death, news of his demise eventually reached the West. Knowing that their leader would be summoned to a *kurultai* in Karakorum, the Mongol horde in Hungary retreated from the front, thus taking the pressure off Europe. Ögedei's wife, Töregene, began her unofficial reign while awaiting the convening of a *kurultai*; during her rule, there was religious friction among her advisors due to the overtaxation that was instituted by her Muslim tax collectors. None of this affected Kublai in his estates, which he ruled with some measure of magnanimity and unusual efficiency. Kublai's mother, the now very powerful Sorghaghtani, allied herself with the regent and Great Khatun Töregene, and it was believed that Sorghaghtani would be her ally in the deliberations of the *kurultai*. The meeting, which was held in 1246, settled the matter of succession to the throne by appointing Ögedei Khan's eldest son, Güyük, to the position.

A picture of the kind of housing that was common among the more elevated of the Mongols was reported on by Friar John of Plano Carpini, in which he described Töregene's tent at Karakorum at the time of the royal meeting. "After five or six days, he [Güyük] sent us to his mother [Empress Töregene], under whom there was maintained a very solemn and royal court. When we came there we saw a huge tent of fine white cloth, which was, in our judgement, so great that more than two thousand men might stand within it, and around about it there was set up a wall of planks, painted with diverse designs." Friar John described the conference of Mongols from as close as he could approach the tent housing the *kurultai*, observing the many dignitaries swarming around the entrance. "Without the door stood Duke Yaroslav of Susdal in Russia, and a great many dukes of the Cathayans, and of the Solands. The two sons also of the King of Georgia, an ambassador of the Caliph of Baghdad, who was a Sultan, and we think, more than ten other Sultans of the Saracens beside."

It is clear that by the time of this conference of royals and major and minor leaders of the Mongol Empire, travel along the Silk Road from had become if not commonplace, at least safe for parties who took the precaution of being accompanied by armed guards. Friar John claimed that some four thousand envoys, speaking many different languages from everywhere in the Mongol Empire, attended the coronation of the new Great Khan Güyük. It took place in a new camp set up some distance from Karakorum. In the center was, according to Friar John, an enormous tent called the Golden Orda. Unfortunately, on the date set for the momentous event, a destructive hailstorm hit, and the ceremonies were called off. A week later, within the confines of the Golden Orda, the princes of the royal family, among whom was Kublai, performed ritual submission before the new great khan. Immediately after the ceremony, Great Khan Güyük, possibly at the behest of his mother, held a show trial in which his aunts were accused of killing his father. They were summarily executed.

Friar John reported his own experience with the wrath of the new khan and his mother. He wrote that the Russian Duke Yaroslav was invited to a banquet with Töregene. "Immediately after the banquet, he fell sick, and within seven days he died. After his death, his body was of a strange blue color, and it was commonly reported that the duke had been poisoned." Accusations were leveled against the perceived enemies of the khan and his mother. It all came to an end when Güyük himself was assassinated or drank himself to death in 1248. It is possible that the great khan was poisoned by his brother Batu, who had been summoned to travel from the west to appear at the court in Karakorum. Any thought of reprisals against the khan's opposition ended with the death of Töregene, who died under suspicious circumstances in 1265, sometime after the enthronement of Kublai Khan.

Batu, who enjoyed his role in the west of the empire, called two *kurultais* of royals to elect a new khan. At the second one in 1251, Sorghaghtani's eldest son, Möngke (r. 1251-1259), was declared to be the great khan. A glimpse of the court of the Great Khan Möngke is given in William of Rubruck's account of his journey to the East. His audience with the great khan did not go well, as Möngke was distracted and drunk throughout their meeting. However, in his explorations of Karakorum, William met some interesting people. Among them was a woman named Paquette who came from Metz in France. She reported to him that she had been captured in Hungary and sent to Karakorum, where she became a slave of a Mongol warrior. She somehow escaped this horror and joined the entourage of a Mongol Christian princess. Paquette later married a Russian carpenter and had three children. William also reported on another Westerner who thrived in Karakorum, a Parisian goldsmith named William Bouchier, who had been captured in Europe and installed by Möngke as the head of a workshop with fifty artisans.

Great Khan Möngke's means of preventing domestic squabbles and revolts among the Mongol factions was to do what the Mongols had always done—conquer new lands. With his eyes on making further conquests in China, Möngke appointed one of his relatives who had shown great skill in pacifying the Chinese. He thus appointed Kublai viceregent over northern China, which Kublai ruled with great acumen, even managing to enlist Chinese warlords to assist him in wars. In 1253, Kublai was ordered to attack Yunnan in southwestern China. In this endeavor, he was remarkably successful. By 1256, he succeeded in pacifying Yunnan and placed it under Mongol control. In 1258, Kublai was put in charge of the eastern Mongol army and ordered to attack Sichuan. His method of approaching the province was unique. The Chinese had depopulated a vast swath of intervening territory so that any invading Mongol force would not be able to pillage enough food to take their army into China. Kublai countered this strategy by encouraging farmers to immigrate into the wasteland, providing them with seed and tools. He sent Chinese soldiers who had willingly joined his army into the fields to assist with the farming. He further instituted the use of paper currency, which facilitated trade along the frontiers and encouraged the migration of farmers into the region.

Kublai planned to defeat the Song Chinese, who were clinging to power in southern China, by outflanking them. In 1253, he moved into the Buddhist mountain kingdom of Dali, which straddled the upper reaches of the Yangtze, Mekong, and Salween Rivers. The Dali Kingdom lay on the major trading route from India to Annam (Vietnam). However, Kublai's envoys to the Dali court, who carried an offer of peace, were killed. According to Mongol custom, this was a capital offense that was deserving of the complete annihilation of the miscreant nation. Kublai was persuaded that this was not a useful approach to the people of Dali, though. Instead, he surrounded the Dali capital and demanded their capitulation. The king surrendered, and Kublai captured those responsible for the killing of his envoys, who were promptly put to death. The king of Dali, being innocent of the crime himself, was spared and left in charge of his city with a Mongol serving as his second-in-command. Kublai moved north from the defeated territory that the Mongols had named Yunnan, meaning south of the clouds. The slow conquest of the scattered hill tribes and the eventual incursion into Tibet was given to Kublai's general Uryangkhadai, who was also responsible for Mongol defeats in Annam (Vietnam). In 1257, Uryangkhadai proceeded as far as Hanoi, where he razed the city to the ground and forced the first emperor of the Trần dynasty, Trần Thái Tông to evacuate the capital. A counterattack led by Thái Tông was successful. The Mongol army, which was depleted by disease in a climate they were unused to, were forced to hurriedly leave Annam. Thái Tông then sent an embassy to the Great Khan Möngke, offering to deliver tribute on an annual basis, which more or less ceded Annam to the Mongols but only in a symbolic way.

Back in his lands in northern China, Kublai continued to follow a somewhat enlightened path, inspired by Chinese practices, in order to establish a stable state. He appointed Confucian scholars to his court and encouraged the hunting down of fortunetellers, who were a scourge according to Confucian orthodoxy. His ability to listen to the advice of his most prominent Confucian advisors and willingness to follow it became suspect in the Mongol capital of Karakorum, where Kublai was thought to be a traitorous Sinophile. He was, however, not entirely seduced by Chinese civilization, as he refused to institute the system of Chinese education and the Chinese system of examinations for positions in the public service. The reason for Kublai's refusal of the Chinese system was that he wanted to retain his Muslim tax collectors and use Nestorian Christian engineers. Further, Kublai would have been leery of heading a bureaucracy where Chinese, a language that he could only master in a rudimentary fashion, was the lingua franca.

When it came to subjugating the entirety of China, Kublai faced two opponents. In the north, the Jurchen people, who had originated in Manchuria and had founded the Jin dynasty. Despite their being conquered in 1234, they continued to present a danger in the form of a revolt. With the Jurchens pacified to a great extent, Kublai only faced the Southern Song in his ambitions to annex all of China into the Mongol Empire.

In order to cement his control over northern China, Kublai proposed building a palace there. A site some 170 miles north of modern Beijing was selected. The site was first named Kaiping, meaning open and flat, but was subsequently changed to Shangdu, or upper capital. The name would be mangled into several variants by Europeans, including Chandu and Xamdu. The latter name metamorphosed into what became the legendary Xanadu. Kublai's remarkable palace is best known to the modern world through the poem by Samuel Taylor Coleridge, written in 1797. It begins, "In Xanadu did Kubla Khan/A stately pleasure-dome decree." Kublai's palace was surrounded by an enormous park, where he exercised his passion for the hunt. In the park, Kublai was in the habit of staying in a yurt, the kind of tent in which his ancestors in Mongolia had lived.

Despite living a high life in his new palace, Kublai was still subservient to Great Khan Möngke. In fact, his accounts were audited by minions of the great khan. Finding irregularities in Kublai's books, several of his Chinese bureaucrats were executed.

Kublai went to his brother Möngke in Karakorum, and their differences were patched up in 1258. Möngke ordered Kublai to stay in his palace at Chandu while Möngke himself moved against the Southern Song at the head of a large army. The invasion did not go well, and Möngke was forced to call in his brother, who he acknowledged as a skilled commander.

At this time, the Mongol court almost collapsed due to infighting between the adherents of rival religions. Their numbers were constantly in flux with the arrivals and departures of religious people who moved along the Silk Road. With the fall of Tibet to Mongol control, Buddhists who were skilled in conjuring tricks seeped into Möngke's and Kublai's courts. They ran afoul of the Chan Buddhists (Zen Buddhists), who were already ensconced in the royal household, and were opposed by Taoists and Confucians, who adamantly opposed anything that smacked of sorcery. In the Mongol courts, on account of a policy of religious tolerance, religious debate was rife. In the 1250s, the Taoists claimed that Buddhism was no more than a sect of their own religion. They bolstered their case by citing the Taoist *Book of Barbarian Conversions*, or the *Huahujing*, which is said to have been written by Laozi, who lived sometime between the 6th to the 4th century BCE. It was said that Laozi traveled to India, where he regenerated into the Buddha. Buddhism was thus seen as merely a deluded form of Taoism. The Buddhist scholars at the great khan's court then backdated Buddha's life so that it predated any possible contact with Laozi, the founder of Taoism, and they declared Buddhism to be the only true religion. The religious dispute had real-world effects with differing religious communities despoiling their opponents' monasteries and temples. Möngke, recognizing Kublai's understanding of the Chinese way of doing things, appointed his brother to convene a debate between the Buddhists and Taoists. In 1258, the religious debate, with Kublai in the judge's chair, was held. Kublai, even though he seems to have adopted a Tibetan named Drogön Chögyal Phagpa as his personal guru, was in favor of the Buddhist argument. With the religious dispute in the Mongol courts settled, the Great Khan Möngke prepared to conquer the Southern Song once and for all. Möngke was to attack the Song from the west, and Kublai was to head south in the winter of 1258/1259 from Chandu with an army of 90,000 men.

In carrying out Genghis Khan's prophecy that the Mongols would rule the entire world, Möngke understood that his expedition would call for a non-Mongolian type of warfare. He enlisted Muslim engineers who had some familiarity with besieging cities in preparation for an attack on the largest urban cities in the world, such as Hangzhou, the temporary capital of the Southern Song, which had a population of around one and half million. While Kublai and his army swept south into Song territory, his brother Möngke got bogged down in fighting in the west. Möngke, although attempting to escape the disease-ridden west, fell victim to cholera and died in 1259 at the age of 51. Going against Mongol custom, which called for a retreat and a subsequent *kurultai* to appoint a new great khan, Kublai opted to continue his advance south across the Yangtze. An emissary from the Song offered to pay off the Mongols with an annual tribute of silver, carpets, fine silks, and brocades if they halted their advance.

At home in Karakorum, Kublai faced opposition. He was forced to retreat from his conquered Song lands and attend the Mongol *kurultai* to ensure that he ascended to the throne of great khan. Two conferences were held in 1260, and Kublai was declared as the next great khan at the first of these. The results were disputed, and a second *kurultai* was convened. The second elected Ariq Bök, Kublai's brother. Kublai's claim was bolstered by the arrival of emissaries from Korea, which was not yet completely subjugated. They swore fealty to Kublai and agreed to dismantle their defenses that had for so long held back Mongol invaders. Without even waging an all-out attack on Korea, Kublai had fortuitously added Korea to the Mongol Empire.

In the first stage of his civil war with his rival, Ariq Bök, for the title of great khan, Kublai cut off the trade routes that ran from Karakorum to the south, which supplied food to the Mongol capital. The dispute reached a climax in 1261 when, on a battlefield at the edge of the Gobi Desert, Ariq Bök's army was defeated by Kublai. The rebellious Bök continued to fight until it became clear to him that Kublai had the upper hand. The two reconciled in Chandu in 1264, but their amity was short-lived. Bök was placed on trial, but it was postponed soon after it started, as it required the attendance of the Mongol princes. Some of them were as far away as the Middle East, but their presence was necessary for a final *kurultai* that would definitively select the great khan. After two years in prison awaiting the convening of a full royal family conference, Bök died. Some suspected he was poisoned. Whatever actually happened, Kublai became the undisputed great khan.

Kublai's court, which had a majority of Chinese bureaucrats and advisors, took on the challenge of how Kublai Khan should rule the Mongol Empire. It may have been Kublai's preferred wife, Chabi, who encouraged him to emulate the administration of the ancient Chinese Tang Empire. Due to their infatuation with Tang China, Kublai and Chabi decided that the best way for the great khan to rule China was not as a Mongol conqueror. Rather, to ensure his hold on the Chinese part of his empire, Kublai would have to "go native" and adopt the Chinese way of government.

Among the allies of Kublai in the invasion of the Southern Song was Li Tan, an official in the Shandong province of Mongolia. He led an army south and was rewarded for his successes by being given the title of vice commander of an area of China the size of modern-day France. Although he was ordered not to move against the Southern Song, Li Tan proved to be victorious in several skirmishes with the Song. He turned against Kublai, who was then preoccupied with Ariq Bök. Li Tan turned his troops loose on the skeletal garrison of Mongols in Shandong and ceded some fortified coastal cities to the Song. Kublai sent two generals to stamp out Li Tan's insurrection, and by the spring of 1262, Li Tan was arrested. It was reported that "When news came to the Great Khan, he was right well pleased, and ordered that all the chiefs who had rebelled, or excited others to rebel, should be put to a cruel death." Li Tan was put in a sack and trampled to death by Mongol horsemen. A confederate of Li Tan and the Song was discovered in Kublai's court, and he, too, was executed. The effect of this rebellion in Shandong was a lessening of the great khan's enthusiasm for the Chinese way of administration. He turned to using officials from non-Chinese cultures, such as the Italian Marco Polo, who took a civil service job in a Chinese city.

Although he may have soured on the Chinese style of government, Kublai understood the importance of the way he managed his Chinese territories. In the north, he wanted to appear sympathetic to Chinese interests so as not to alarm the Song Chinese, who were on the verge of being forced into the Mongol Empire. The management of the Chinese needed to be handled delicately because, in the north, the Mongols were outnumbered, perhaps by a margin of five to one. If Kublai assumed control of southern China, with a population in the range of forty million, the scarcity of Mongols to keep order would become critical. So, he set about putting advice from his Confucian advisors into practice. They proposed that Kublai always present a magnanimous face. If he was effective in winning the hearts and minds of the Song, they would, without warfare, beg to be permitted to enter the Mongol Empire.

An emissary was sent by Kublai to the Song, who pleaded for their complete submission to Mongol authority. The ambassador painted Kublai as a virtual Chinese man who would make few changes to the organization of the Song bureaucracy. The most important difference would be that taxes would flow to the great khan and not the leader of the Song Empire. Kublai promised to ensure that Song merchants would not be harassed in the north, insisting that their trade route would continue as it had in the past when the north was under Chinese domination. In spite of this, there were continual tensions on the Yangtze River, the border between the Mongols and the Song. It was actually Kublai's Mongol heart, full as it was with traditional Mongol expansionist notions, that won him over. Kublai prepared for a major invasion of the south, following the Mongol tradition of expansionism to generate wealth, to gather new slaves to put to work, and to focus the attention of subjects on outward goals. It was his intention to settle dealings with the Song by taking over their territory.

The invasion of the south involved a difficult transition in the Mongol means of warfare. While Kublai's army was adept on the flatlands of the steppes, they were untrained in slogging through the wet rice fields of the south, surviving intense heat, and fending off tropical diseases. The challenge of finding enough grazing land for the Mongol horses and the unprecedented need to deal with shipborne fighters that were fielded by the Song weighed heavily on Kublai Khan. In order to cross the Yangtze effectively and to patrol the coastline of Song China, Kublai needed a navy. The beginning of this enterprise was the capture of 146 Song ships that had sailed up the Yangtze almost as far as Sichuan. These ships were put to use by Kublai in his attack in 1268 on Xiangyang (in the modern-day Hubei province) on the Han River. Even though it was surrounded by Mongol forts, food and soldiers made it into the city, providing relief for the inhabitants inside. The siege went on and on. A major delivery of supplies to the besieged city came when two thousand Song soldiers smashed the Mongol blockade on the Han River. The Mongol siege was, in a sense, professionalized when experts in siege warfare arrived from Persia. These engineers built huge trebuchets, or mangonels, that were capable of throwing a 300-pound rock over the walls of the city. Using these devices, the Mongols pounded the walls of Xiangyang into rubble. The historical sources are unclear as to whether the builders of the mangonels were, in fact, Persians. One source claims the engineers were from Damascus, where familiarity with the effectiveness of mangonels was obtained from the sieges of Crusader castles. In his book about his visit to Kublai Khan, the Italian merchant Marco Polo went so far as to claim that the mangonel builders were himself, his father, his uncle, and some unnamed assistants. "Then spoke up the two brothers and Messer Marco the son, and said: 'Great Prince, we have with us among our followers men who are able to construct mangonels which shall cast such great stones that the garrison will never be able to stand them, but surrender." The boasting of this deed has much to do with Polo's entire account of his stay in China being seen as a false narrative. When the siege of Xiangyang occurred, the Polos were not even in China.

Xiangyang finally fell to the Mongols in 1272 after a five-year siege. In order to consolidate the command of his expeditionary force, Kublai appointed General Bayan to be the supreme commander. He marched his troops down the Yangtze and laid siege to Hangzhou. His army was bolstered with the addition of many Song Chinese turncoats who understood that trade with the Mongols would eventually be conducted with respect.

The Song Chinese, at the time of the siege, were led by Empress Dowager Quan and Grand Empress Dowager Xie. The latter was a very strong advocate for the Song cause; at one point, she egged on her supporters, proclaiming, "Since ancient times there has not yet been an age of total barbarian conquest. How has it come to this present state that deviates from the constants of Heaven and Earth."

In spite of her bluster, at the end of 1275, Xie was forced to turn over the imperial seal to Bayan, ceding the Song capital to him. The four-year-old heir to the Song dynasty was packed off to the south. He was eventually apprehended by the Mongols and sent to a monastery in Tibet.

Even before the fall of Hangzhou, Kublai declared himself to be the emperor of China. He chose the name for his dynasty carefully so as not to emphasize its "barbarian" origin and antagonize the population. So, in a brilliant move, he established the Yuan dynasty. Kublai sent letters to the peoples on the periphery of his new Chinese empire. From the king of Korea, he received strong support since the Mongol troops had been instrumental in putting down an insurrection against the king. He wrote to the Japanese and the king of Annam, expecting them to swiftly acknowledge his role as Ruler of All Under Heaven. In both cases, the authorities dragged their feet.

Meanwhile, the great khan busied himself in creating a capital fit for the new emperor of China.

Chapter 9 – Marco Polo Visits Kublai Khan's China

While conquering the southern Chinese and subsequently founding the Yuan Dynasty in 1279, Kublai Khan had to deal with unrest in the far reaches of his empire. In Mongolia, he was constantly threatened by internal warfare. In the west of the Mongol Empire, unrest swept the rulership of the Golden Horde. Kublai's administrators were pushed aside in a civil war, and the armies of the Golden Horde and those of the Mongol khanate in Persia, known as the Ilkhanate, clashed. In this period of internal strife, traders from the Latin West made inroads in commerce with nearby parts of the Mongol Empire. By 1263, western merchants were established in Tabriz, the leading commercial center of Persia. Under Hulagu Khan, the ruler of the Ilkhanate from 1256 to 1265, and his successor Abaqa Khan, who reigned from 1265 to 1282, the relations between the Christian West and Persia improved. Abaqa had a Christian mother, and among his wives was the daughter of Byzantine Emperor Michael VIII Palaeologus. This meant that Christian missionaries, diplomats, and merchants became prominent in the city of Tabriz. Attempts were made to improve diplomacy between the court of Abaqa and the West, among which was the failed coordination of Persian military action and the Crusade of Prince Edward of England between 1270 and 1272.

The primary source of information on what lay to the east of Europe during the first half of the 14th century was a book entitled *The Travels of Marco Polo* or the *Book of the Marvels of the World*, dating from around 1300. Most of what surrounds this account of Polo's journey to the East is shrouded in mystery, and the truth of its contents has been subject to debate.

In the 1250s, Venetian merchants Niccolò and Maffeo Polo ran a trading business shipping goods from the East to Venice, where they were then transported to European markets. The Polos operated out of the Crimean port of Soldaia (modern-day Sudak). Their major competition came from Venetian trading enterprises operating from Constantinople, which was the center of the Latin Empire, which stretched from the Balkans to the Levant. Among the exotic trade goods that flowed from the East into Constantinople and dependent ports were silk, dyes, furs, pepper, cotton, and slaves. It was to Crimea that Russians delivered amber, honey, wax, and furs. The most important of the Polos trade was in foodstuffs originating in the European steppes.

According to the book that became known as *The Travels of Marco Polo*, Niccolò and Maffeo Polo set out in 1260 to trade jewels with the merchants of the Golden Horde in Russia. They traveled to Sarai (near present-day Volgograd), where they met and exchanged goods with the grandson of Genghis Khan, Berke Khan, who reigned over the Golden Horde from 1257 to 1266. Because the archenemy of Venice, Genoa, in league with the Byzantines, reconquered Constantinople in 1261, the Polos avoided returning to Venice through Byzantine territory. They might have wished to travel south from Russia through Georgia and Armenia to Tabriz, the capital of the Ilkhanate, but this route home became impossible because a war had broken out between Berke Khan of the Golden Horde and Hulagu, the Mongol khan of Persia. Apparently, the Polos left Sarai and headed directly east, crossing a desert in central

Asia to arrive at Bukhara, located in present-day Uzbekistan. There, they were convinced by an emissary from the Persian Ilkhan Hulagu, who was on his way to see the great khan, that they should join him. According to the book, the Polo brothers traveled a year north and northeast until they arrived at the court of Kublai Khan.

The great khan gave them letters in Mongolian to deliver to the pope. He asked the pope to send him one hundred teachers of the liberal arts who could convert the Mongols to Catholicism. The actual nature of this request seems to have been more along the lines of the great khan needing the assistance of European administrators to deal with the Chinese in the north, who Kublai was on the verge of conquering. Kublai Khan also asked that the Polos secure for him some oil from the lamp of the Holy Sepulcher in Jerusalem and have it sent to him. To facilitate their journey west to their home in Venice, the Polo brothers were given a pass that entitled them to pass through all of the Mongol lands without hindrance. After a journey that was said, although most likely in exaggeration, to have lasted three years, they reached the port of Layas or Aegeae (now the Turkish holiday town of Yumurtalik) and sailed off to Acre and from there sailed home to Venice. In Venice, Niccolò was reunited with his son Marco, who the book says was fifteen years old at the time.

Three years later, the Polo brothers decided to visit the great khan, and they took Niccolò's young son Marco with them. They sailed to Acre and then visited Jerusalem to secure the sacred oil as requested by the great khan. Returning to Acre, they learned that Archdeacon Tedaldo Visconti, then in residence there, had just been elected as Pope Gregory X (pontiff from 1271 to 1276).

The new pope, instead of sending a group of educators or administrators to Kublai Khan as requested, provided the Polo merchant expedition with two Dominican friars, Brother Niccolò of Vicenza and Brother William of Tripoli. They were, according to *The Travels of Marco Polo*, endowed by the pope with "the necessary authority, that they might do everything in those countries with full powers, ordain priests and consecrate bishops...He [the pope] gave them written credentials and letters, and entrusted them with the message he wished to send to the Great Khan." The journey to the court of the great khan took three and a half years, which Marco Polo said was "owing to the bad weather and severe cold they encountered." They arrived in Karakorum in 1275. There, they "went to the Royal Palace, where they found the Great Khan surrounded by a large company of barons. So, they kneeled before him and paid him their respects in the humblest possible manner...They presented the credentials and letters the Pope sent him, which pleased him exceedingly. They then consigned the holy oil, over which he rejoiced very much."

Marco described Kublai Khan in the book, saying, "He is of good stature, neither tall nor short, but of a middle height. He has a becoming amount of flesh, and is very shapely in all his limbs. His complexion is white and red, the eyes black and fine, the nose well formed and well set on."

The Polos were to spend the next seventeen years in the East. Although there are no Chinese records to confirm this, according to the record of the Polos' travels, Kublai Khan used young Marco as an administrator.

> Now it happened that Marco, the son of Messer Niccolò, learnt so well the customs, languages and manners of writing of the Tartars, that it was truly a wonder, for I tell you in sooth that, not long after he had reached the Court of the Great Lord, he knew four languages, and their alphabets, and manner of writing. He was exceedingly wise and prudent, and the Great Khan loved him very much.

In 1273, Kublai completed his conquest of China, thus reuniting both northern and southern China. Marco Polo seems to have served the great khan as an ambassador to far-off regions of the Mongol Empire, reporting back with descriptions of the peoples and what he saw. The Polos, who had asked permission to return to Europe on several occasions but were rebuffed by the great khan, were at last chosen to accompany an imperial princess on her journey to marry Arghun Khan. After an arduous voyage, the princess was delivered to the khan's court in Persia. The three Polos traveled west through Trebizond on the Black Sea to Constantinople and arrived home in Venice in 1295. Marco was, at the time, 41 or 42 years of age.

At some point, under circumstances that are unknown, Marco was captured at sea by the Genoese. He was thrown into prison where, apparently, he wrote the account of his travels to the East. Marco was released and, in 1299, returned home to Venice. Marco's manuscript for his book on his travels was copied by scribes and translated into several European languages, and Marco was consulted by scholars on the subjects of geography and the peoples of the East.

The co-author of *The Travels of Marco Polo*, Rustichello da Pisa, was with Marco in prison in Genoa. The flourishes of romance included in the travel book and the way the story is framed have been attributed to Rustichello. It is for this reason that one should doubt every statement in the book as being entirely factual. Scholars have debated whether indeed the book was dictated by Marco Polo himself, and they have also disputed over the input of copyists of the text, as the original has disappeared. Furthermore, scholars have found it difficult to determine the locations of many of the places mentioned in the text. It is believed that Marco Polo and Rustichello da Pisa often used place names that were poorly translated from local languages. Considering some of Polo's observations, whether accurate or not, is valuable in understanding what kind of information was spread in Europe regarding the previously unrecorded path to the East and the wonders of China.

Marco Polo described the city of Mosul as he observed it in the late 13th century. He reported that in Mongol-controlled Mosul, Christians of various sects and Muslims intermingled freely. He noted that the Muslims manufactured silk cloths and that they "convey spices and drugs, in large quantities, from one country to another." In the mountains north of Mosul, said Polo, "there is a race of people named Kurds...They are an unprincipled people, whose occupation is to rob merchants."

In Baghdad, the Venetian merchant wrote, that "there is a manufacture of silks wrought with gold, and also of damasks, as well as of velvets ornamented with figures of birds and beasts." In Taurus in Iraq, "the inhabitants support themselves principally by commerce and manufactures, which latter consist of various kinds of silk, some of them interwoven with gold, and of high price." From this, we can learn that silk, perhaps even the bulk of it, moving along the Silk Road to the West was not manufactured by the Chinese. Taurus was an important trading center, where, "The merchants from India...as well as from different parts of Europe, resort thither to purchase and sell a number of articles." As a good Christian, Marco Polo could not resist opining on the Muslims, the dominant group of Taurus. He said that according to their doctrine, whatever was stolen or plundered from others of a different faith was now theirs, and the theft would be not be seen as a crime.

While in Persia, Marco Polo inquired the locals about the origin of the three Magi, who brought exotic gifts to the infant Jesus. He recorded the story in his book, along with other regional legends. He encountered Yazidis in Persia and noted that they made "a species of cloth of silk and gold...known by the appellation of Yasti." This cloth was "carried from thence by the merchants to all parts of the world." Marco Polo tells of the city-state of Ormus (Hormuz), where the temperatures forced the inhabitants to retreat in the summer to houses that had been constructed over a river. This was probably hearsay that Marco Polo had obtained through imperfect translation. It is likely that this reference to houses on a river, in fact, concerned the forced evacuation of the people of Ormuz to the island of Hormuz, who were pushed out by the Muslim Kerman Seljuk Sultanate or by the Mongol invaders.

In Timochain, located in the Fars Province of northern Persia, Marco Polo records that he learned of the legend of the Old Man of the Mountain, including his band of assassins and his base in the city of Balach that was destroyed by the Mongols. Balach, says Marco Polo, "contained many palaces constructed of marble, and spacious squares, still visible, although in a ruinous state." In this part of the story of his travels, Marco Polo describes Kashmir, although it is unlikely that he went there.

Reaching Kotan on the southern route of the Silk Road around the Taklamakan Desert, Marco Polo says that the people there were mostly Muslims. We know today that Polo's observation was incorrect because Khotan was, at the time, a Buddhist state within the Mongol Empire. Khotan, said Polo, "yields cotton, flax, hemp, grain, wine and other articles. The inhabitants cultivate farms and vineyards and have numerous gardens. They support themselves also by trade and manufactures, but they are not good soldiers."

When he came to the Lop Desert, in what is today the home of the Muslim Uyghurs in Xinjiang in the far northwest of China, Polo records that the region, which was under the dominion of the great khan, was populated with Muslims. Travelers who intended to cross the desert, said Polo, "usually halt for a considerable time at this place [the town of Lop], as well to repose from their fatigues as to make the necessary preparations for their further journey. For this purpose, they load a number of stout asses and camels with provisions and with their merchandise...Camels are commonly here employed in preference to asses, because they carry heavy burdens and are fed with a small quantity of provisions. The stock of provisions should be laid in for a month, that time being required for crossing the desert in the narrowest part."

In the part of his tale when Polo gets to Karakorum, the former capital of the Mongol Empire, he relates the story of how Genghis Khan marched against Prester John, who was encamped on the great plain of Tenduk. After receiving good omens for the outcome of the battle, the Mongols launched an attack. The Mongol army broke through Prester John's ranks and entirely routed the enemy.

"Prester John himself was killed, his kingdom fell to the conqueror, and Genghis Khan espoused his daughter."

The Great Khan's palace in Shandu (Chandu or Xanadu), says Polo, had halls and chambers all in gilt. The palace was "contained within a wall to enclose sixteen miles in circuit of the adjoining plain. It contains the Royal Park with trees and birds. The number of these birds is upwards of two hundred, without counting the hawks." In the midst of the park, there was a royal pavilion in the form of a yurt.

> It is gilt all over, most elaborately finished inside and decorated with beasts and birds of very skillful workmanship. It is supported upon a colonnade of handsome pillars, gilt and varnished. Round each pillar a dragon, likewise gilt, entwines its tail, whilst its head sustains the projection of the roof, and its talons or claws are extended to the left and right...The construction of the pavilion is so devised that it can be taken down and put up again quickly; and it can be taken to pieces and removed wherever the Emperor may command. When erected, it is braced by more than 200 chords of silk.

Polo then gives a description of Kublai's successful battle against the rebellious Mongol Prince Nayan. This may be a firsthand report of the event that took place in July of 1287. "Kublai took his station in a large wooden castle, borne on the backs of four elephants, whose bodies were protected with coverings of thick leather hardened by fire, over which were housings of cloth of gold. The castle contained many crossbow-men and archers." In *The Travels of Marco Polo*, Kublai Khan's army is said to have "consisted of thirty battalions of horse, each battalion containing ten thousand men." After his victory, Kublai Khan returned to Khanbalu (Beijing) in November.

At Easter the following year, Kublai Khan told the Christians to "attend to him" and to bring their Bible. Marco Polo recorded the following about it in his book.

After causing it [the Bible] to be repeatedly perfumed with incense, in a ceremonious manner, he devoutly kissed it, and directed that the same should be done by all his nobles who were present. This was his usual practice upon each of the principal Christian festivals...He observed the same at the festivals of the Saracens [Muslims], Jews and idolaters. Upon being asked his motive for this conduct, he said: "There are four great Prophets who are reverenced and worshipped by the different classes of mankind...I do honor and show respect to all four"...But from the manner in which his majesty acted toward them, it is evident that he regarded the faith of the Christians as the right one and the best; nothing, as he observed, being enjoined to its professors that was not filled with virtue and holiness.

Whether this was true or not, it should be understood that Polo was writing for a Christian audience.

One of the customs of the great khan that clearly astonished Marco Polo involved his choice of marital partners.

When his majesty is desirous of the company of one of his empresses, he either sends for her, or goes himself to her palace. Besides these, he has many concubines provided for his use from a province of Tartary named Ungut [possibly in modern-day Iran], the inhabitants of which are distinguished for beauty of features and fairness of complexion. Every second year, or oftener, as it may happen to be his pleasure, the Great Khan sends thither his officers, who collect for him, one hundred or more, of the handsomest of the young women, according to the estimation of beauty communicated to them in their instructions.

Marco Polo was present during the construction of Kublai Khan's royal palace and Chinese capital in Beijing. One of the buildings that impressed him was an observatory constructed in the 1270s.

They have a kind of astrolabe on which are inscribed the planetary signs, the hours and critical points of the whole year. Every year the Christian, Saracen and Chinese astrologers, each sect apart, investigate by means of this astrolabe the course and character of the whole year...in order to discover by the natural course and disposition of the planets, and the other circumstances of the heavens...what shall be the nature of the weather, and what peculiarities shall be produced by each Moon of the year.

This astonishing scientific procedure was something quite foreign in Europe, and thus it fascinated the visiting Marco Polo. He was likewise in awe over the great khan's project for his new capital, saying that "All the plots of ground on which the houses of the city are built are four-square and laid out with straight lines...Each square plot [in Beijing] is encompassed by handsome streets for traffic, and thus the whole city is arranged in squares just like a chess-board." This was, of course, nothing like the medieval cities of Europe, where topography and traditional paths determined the siting of housing plots. Marco Polo left Beijing before the renovation and extension of the Grand Canal, linking Beijing and Hangzhou, was completed. This engineering feat would certainly have impressed him. Marco Polo also missed the completion of the elaborate system of water supply and lake extension in the north of the city. Because no Westerner would have been allowed within a stone's throw of Kublai's palace itself, it was only described by those who climbed a hill overlooking the structure. Friar Odoric of Pordenone, who visited Beijing after Marco Polo, wrote of the palace in rather vague terms. "In the city, the great emperor Khan has his principal seat, and his imperial palace, the walls of which palace are four miles in circuit." One of Kublai's major contributions to the cityscape of Beijing was the restoration of the 11th-century Great White Pagoda. This Buddhist structure was the tallest building in Beijing.

The objects of trade that reached Beijing were all subject to the monopoly of the great khan. Marco Polo noted the following:

> Furthermore, all merchants arriving from India or other countries, and bringing with them gold or silver or gems and pearls, are prohibited from selling to any one but the Emperor. He has twelve experts chosen for this business, men of shrewdness and experience in such affairs; these appraise the articles, and the Emperor then pay a liberal price for them in those pieces of paper [paper currency].

While Kublai was not the first to use paper currency, his use of this kind of commerce was widespread enough to intrigue Marco Polo. He reported that the money was made from the tough bark of the mulberry tree and was treated with great respect. It was a legal tender whose use was enforced by the law. If a merchant refused to accept it as payment, he was subject to execution. When notes became too damaged to be used, merchants could swap them at the imperial treasury on payment of a 3 percent fee.

Marco Polo said of the khan's finances, "Now you have heard the ways and means whereby the Great Khan may have, and in fact has, more treasure than all the Kings in the World; and you know all about it and the reason why." Of course, the use of paper money inevitably resulted in inflation.

There was, at this time, other contacts established between the East and the West. Under the patronage of Kublai Khan, two Nestorian monks, Rabban Sauma and Rabban Mark, undertook a pilgrimage west to Jerusalem. Both of these monks were of Turkish or Uyghur origin. Their route took them along the Silk Road, passing Khotan, Kashgar, and Azerbaijan, and arriving in Baghdad in 1280. Here, the patriarch of the Nestorian Church appointed Rabban Mark as the Nestorian Metropolitan of Cathay and Ong (Shanxi). When the patriarch died, Rabban Mark was appointed, probably at the command of Kublai Khan, to be the new patriarch of the Nestorian Church. Rabban Sauma, in 1287, was sent on by Arghun Khan to head an embassy to Europe. He was accompanied by two Italians, Tommaso, a member of a Genoese banking family, and Ughetto, who was to act as an interpreter. They went to Rome and Genoa, met with King Philip IV in Paris, and celebrated Christian communion with Edward I of England in Bordeaux. Rabban Sauma went back to Rome, where he met with Pope Nicholas IV and delivered an invitation from Arghun Khan to send Catholic missionaries to the court of the Great Khan Kublai.

The pope commissioned the Franciscan friar John of Montecorvino to travel to China in response to Kublai Khan's request. John set out in 1289 in the company of Dominican Friar Nicholas of Pistoia and a merchant, Peter of Lucalongo. It was clearly the intention that land-based commerce along the Silk Road would be an important byproduct of converting the Chinese. The mission followed a circuitous route to the court of the great khan. After stopping in Tabriz, the capital of the Ilkhanate in Persia, Montecorvino and his companions sailed to Madras in India in 1291. He then went by sea from Bengal to China, where he appeared in Khanbaliq (modern-day Beijing) in 1294. Although Kublai Khan had died and the Mongol Empire was ruled by his successor, Temür Khan (r. 1294–1307), John was welcomed by the new great khan and the rulers of the Chinese puppet state of the Mongols known as the Yuan dynasty.

John built two churches in Khanbaliq and set up Christian workshops, which he populated with young boys he had bought from their heathen parents. He had the boys instructed in Latin and Greek and trained them in the rites and traditions of the Catholic Church. He taught himself the Uyghur language, which was the common tongue of the Mongol rulers in China, and translated the New Testament and Psalms into Uyghur. John's success involved the conversion of hundreds of Chinese-Mongols and earned him the wrath of Nestorian Christians, who were quite numerous in the territories controlled by the Mongols in Yuan China. Christian reinforcements were sent to John in 1307, but of the seven Franciscans who set out from Europe, only three arrived in China.

As instructed by the pope, they consecrated John as the archbishop of Beijing. Among the high points reported in John's mission was the conversion of the great khan to Catholicism, who, at the time, was Külüg (r. 1307–1311) and known as Emperor Wuzong of the Yuan dynasty. However, there is some doubt as to the truth of this claim. It is thought that John of Montecorvino died in Beijing around 1328 because, in a letter from 1336 from Toghon Temür, who became the emperor of the Yuan dynasty in 1333, it was reported that the Chinese Mongol khanate had lacked a spiritual leader for the eight years since John's death. The letter was delivered by an embassy sent from Mongol China headed by Andrea di Nascio, a Genoese in the court of Toghon Temür. Di Nascio was accompanied by another Genoese merchant, Andalò di Savignone. The presence of trusted Genoese in the court in China indicates that by this time, there was significant commerce between the East and the West.

The pope maintained an interest in the affairs of the Christian Church in China. In 1338, he sent fifty ecclesiastics to the Mongol khanate in China. The absence of religious prejudice among the Mongols allowed for the prosperity of the Christian Church in Yuan China. This all came to an end, though, in 1368, when the Chinese rose up and overthrew their Mongol overlords. In the early years of the Ming dynasty, which lasted from 1368 to 1644, all of the Christians were expelled from China.

Marco Polo, throughout his many travels, visited many large and small cities in Yuan China. Most of those named in his book cannot be connected with any degree of certainty to specific Chinese cities. One that can, however, is Kin Sai, which has been identified as Hangzhou, which, it is said, that Marco Polo visited frequently. Hangzhou, it is stated, is a hundred miles in circumference, "its streets and canals are extensive, and there are squares and market-places...[where] officers appointed by the Great Khan are stationed, to take immediate notice of any differences that may happen to arise between the foreign merchants..." Canals "run through every quarter of the city" and are crossed by twelve thousand bridges. Around part of the city was a ditch that served to divert flooding rivers and functioned as a defensive moat when necessary. Marco Polo was impressed by the markets of Hangzhou, which he described in detail, noting, in particular, the delicious peaches and pears. He also seems to have been attracted by the courtesans who lived in a special quarter of Hangzhou. "These women," he said, "are accomplished, and are perfect in the arts of caressing and fondling which they accompany with expressions adapted to every description of person."

The extensive description of Hangzhou and its inhabitants by Marco Polo suggests that it was his favorite of all the cities he visited in China. He took great interest in the recreation afforded by the lake in Hangzhou, describing in detail the vessels in which the locals amused themselves "either in the company of their women or that of their male companions." The people of Hangzhou, said Marco Polo, "think of nothing else" after their days of labor than "passing the remaining hours in parties of pleasure, with their wives or their mistresses."

Chapter 10 – The Final Years of Kublai Khan

The defeat of the remaining Song came about in a naval battle near Xinhui (in modern-day Guangdong) in the Battle of Yamen, which was fought on March 19th, 1279. With the demise of the remnants of the Song administration, Kublai Khan could, in truth, claim to be the emperor of a China that was unified for the first time in centuries. Rather than attempt to expand Mongol rule in the south into Vietnam, Kublai Khan turned his attention to Japan, the most important kingdom in the Far East that had yet to fall under Mongol control.

In his plan to subjugate Japan, the kingdom of Korea had to be called upon to provide military resources. This was the price that King Wonjong (ruled off and on between 1260 and 1274) had to pay for agreeing to subject his country to Mongol authority. Thus, he and his successors served as the great khan's agents in fighting with Japan. After a series of raids on Japan and preemptive attacks by Japan on the coast of Korea, Kublai sent an embassy to Japan in 1266, demanding that the nation submit to the Ruler of the World. He also sent a letter to King Wonjong of Korea, demanding that Korean warriors act as his proxies in an invasion of Japan. The

Koreans obfuscated, though, and Kublai responded with a demand that they cooperate with his expansionist plan. He wrote to the king of Korea, "As to the Japanese matter, we shall leave it entirely in your hands, and we desire your Highness to bide by our wishes and convey our message to Japan, resting only when the end is attained without mishap." He also wrote to the emperor of Japan, who he addressed as "the king of a little country," saying, "We desire to remind you that Korea is now one of our eastern provinces, and that Japan is a mere appendage of Korea." This letter was ignored, as were representatives from Korea. A Korean ambassador to Kublai's court attempted to dissuade the great khan from his designs on Japan. Kublai said that the Japanese were presumptuous, even to the level of calling their leader emperor of the Land of the Rising Sun. Further, said the ambassador, the rumor that Japan was extraordinarily wealthy was, in fact, overblown. His last piece of advice to the great khan outlined the difficulties and dangers of a seaborne assault on Japan. The ambassador was doing his best to protect the interests of Korea, as it was expected that any Mongol invasion of Japan would be carried out, for the most part, by Korean mariners and soldiers. He failed to convince Kublai, though, who ordered that Korea construct one thousand ships and fill them with four thousand bags of rice and man them with forty thousand troops.

After sending three missions to Japan, none of which got farther than the island of Tsushima in the Korean Strait, Kublai sent a trusted advisor to Japan. Upon reading the great khan's demand that Japan subject itself to his authority, the ambassador was ejected from Japan. Kublai might well have abandoned his designs on Japan, but the arrogance of the Japanese in rejecting any notion of friendship with the Yuan emperor of China, coupled with the need in the Mongol Empire to project absolute strength, forced Kublai to invade Japan.

In 1274, a fleet of Korean ships carrying fifteen thousand Korean, Mongol, and Jurchen soldiers set out from the port of Pusan. The armada stopped at the island of Tsushima and launched an assault on the local samurai. The samurai, who were trained to conduct war in a ritual fashion, soon fell to the Mongol assault of poisoned arrows and ungentlemanly mass violence. The samurai, overwhelmed by the superior numbers, retreated, and they, along with the civilian inhabitants of Tsushima, were massacred. The same thing happened when the massive fleet landed on the island of Iki. To throw terror into the hearts of those on the sparsely defended island, the ships had their prows decorated with the captured dead or dying naked women, whose bodies, according to the annals of the Yuan dynasty, were affixed with nails through their palms. Pushing their lines forward behind a mass of captured Japanese women, the Mongols succeeded in overtaking the entire island.

The Mongol fleet soon moved on to Hakata Bay on the island of Kyūshū, a natural place for an amphibious assault. The samurai on this island were better prepared than those of the other Japanese islands. The Japanese knights held back the Mongol onslaught, and the Mongol forces retreated to their ships at the end of the day's fighting. A conference aboard the Mongol flagship was indecisive of whether the Japanese would attack before moonrise and whether the Mongols should mount a counterattack on land immediately. The samurai struck first. In more than three hundred tiny boats, they surrounded the Mongol fleet and pushed fireboats against the enemy ships. Fire on the vessels, whose holds had been kept dry to preserve gunpowder, spread quickly, and some vessels exploded. The Mongol ship captains attempted to move their vessels out to the open sea, where they expected to be able to ride out the destructive storm that had suddenly moved into Hakata Bay. However, the Mongol fleet was destroyed in the violent storm, with only a few ships surviving to retreat to Korea. What became known as the Battle of Bun'ei or the First Battle of Hakata Bay on

November 19th, 1274, became the stuff of legend in Japan, as the victory over the Mongols was attributed not only to the superiority of the samurai warriors but also to divine intervention with the arrival of a storm at a critical moment in the conflict.

Following the Mongol defeat, Kublai Khan sent an emissary to Japan. The ambassador made the mistake of calling the Japanese emperor a king and said that the leader of the Mongols was a great emperor. Emperor Hōjō Tokimune (r. 1268-1284) dismissed the Mongol offer of peace. He said in no uncertain terms to Kublai's ambassador, "Listen, Mongol. Whosoever threatens a peaceful nation or tribe with the object of confiscating its resources...is without doubt a robber." And he added that since the time of Genghis Khan, "not a single day has been spent in peaceful rule, but the east and west have been terrorized by the Khan's brutal acts." The audience went from bad to worse, and the envoys of Kublai were executed. It is likely that Emperor Tokimune's fierce resistance to the Mongols was a result of the unrest in Japan caused by a popular Buddhist sect foretelling the end of the world. This doomsday prognostication was something that the bravest of samurai would have thought to be unthinkable.

Because the murder of ambassadors was anathema to the Mongol code of ethics, Kublai sent out orders to Korea that a second armada must be prepared. A further directive was delivered to Kublai's administrators in Yangzhou on the Grand Canal. One of the public servants in Yangzhou was Marco Polo, and he recorded the massive undertaking there to construct fifteen thousand ships "to carry his [the great khan's] armies to the isles of the sea." He said that each of the transport ships would have a crew of twenty and carry fifteen horses with their riders and provisions. It was through the writings of Marco Polo that the West first learned of Japan, although he called the country "Cipangu" and what he said of it was entirely based on Kublai's invasion. Working from imperial Mongol propaganda, Polo stated that Japan was a country of immense wealth, having much gold and pearls in abundance. The Japanese emperor's palace was, said Polo, "entirely roofed with fine gold," and the floors throughout the palace were paved in gold "in plates like slabs of stone, a good two fingers thick."

The Yangzhou fleet under the command of the Mongol general Arkham and the Korean fleet left their home ports in June 1281. When they finally met up in Hakata Bay in August, the fighters, which included Koreans, Mongols, and Chinese, were in poor condition on account of disease and exhaustion. Their supplies were dwindling, and their vessels were subject to almost continuous harassment by little Japanese boats with samurai fighters on board. The stalemate would have continued for some time, were it not for a major tempest that struck the Tsushima Straits on August 15th. The two-day storm destroyed almost all of the Mongol fleet. The Japanese reported that over four thousand ships went down. Recent studies by marine archaeologists suggest that the ships built in Yangzhou were, in haste, improperly constructed and thus unable to withstand violent seas.

Kublai immediately sent out orders for the preparation of a third attack on Japan. These orders, however, were rescinded when the great khan became preoccupied with dissent within his empire. The most significant outcome of the two failed invasions of Japan was the now apparent fact that the Mongols were not, as previously believed, invincible.

The later years of Kublai's reign were distinguished by attempts to bolster his administration in areas of strategic importance. He appointed a Muslim governor for Yunnan in southern China in order to exercise tight control over the roads to Annam and Mian (Burma). The origins of the governor reveal the thinking of the great khan when it came to ensuring that his empire was properly managed by loyal administrators. Sayyid Ajall Shams al-Din Omar (1211–1279) was a Khwarezmian Muslim from Bukhara (in modern-day Uzbekistan). He had served in the army of Kublai and

Möngke, and he had been instrumental in the conquest of the Kingdom of Dali in 1274. Sayyid excelled in Yunnan because, as an outsider, he was respected for his fair treatment of the people of the province. During his tenure, public works were improved with the institution of water conservation projects, irrigation works, and construction of terraces for gardens. Sayyid also built mosques, Confucian temples and schools, and a Buddhist monastery. After he died, his policies were continued by his sons. In short, under Sayyid, the Yuan province thrived, and the trade along paths leading to Southeast Asia expanded. While most of the trade between the West and Burma and Vietnam was a maritime enterprise, it is not unlikely that goods from the region traveled north by land to the ancient Silk Road and thence westward.

The kind of religious toleration and economic prosperity in Yunnan that was favored by Kublai did not exist for long in Beijing and other parts of the Mongol Empire. When Taoists in Beijing set a Buddhist monastery on fire in 1280, Kublai was forced to take action in what had been a long-simmering conflict. He ordered that copies of the Taoist *Book of Barbarian Conversions* be hunted down and destroyed. Although Kublai had previously made a similar prohibition against the book, it was not entirely effective, so he also ordered the destruction of all printing blocks that were used in making multiple copies of the book. Kublai's wrath fell heavily on uneducated and untrained ersatz Taoists who made their living offering services of divination, soothsaying, and other esoteric practices.

A further religious conflict erupted over the Muslim practice of *halal*, or permissible butchering. The practice was contrary to the Mongol custom of butchering animals, as they drained the blood prior to cutting apart the animal. It was these kinds of disputes that began to erupt in Kublai's court, which had been built so as to be all-inclusive with respect to religions. In the aftermath of the *halal* controversy, Muslims in the imperial administration were attacked by Buddhists and Taoists, and they fell victim to prejudice among the Chinese population who resented the authority of non-Chinese, regardless of their religion.

As Kublai aged, the question of what religion he preferred became more and more urgent. His fence-sitting stance on contending religions became less an attribute to be admired and more a thorn in his side. Kublai's appointment of his second son Zhenjin as his heir apparent in 1283 exacerbated the conflicts among religious leaders vying for power in the empire. Zhenjin was first educated by Confucian scholars before falling under the influence of a Tibetan Buddhist, Drogön Chögyal Phagpa, who is said to have written the book *What One Should Know* for the benefit of the young prince. It became a matter of urgency in the imperial court as to which religion Kublai's successor might favor. Nestorian Christians began to lose their authority, and Catholicism was a non-starter, so it was a toss-up whether Zhenjin would tend to be more sympathetic to Islam, Buddhism, Confucianism, or Taoism. Any currying of the favor of Zhenjin by religious leaders was not to bear fruit since Zhenjin died in 1286 at the age of 43.

Kublai's reign was thrust into turmoil in the years after the 1281 assassination of Ahmad Fanākati, who was one of his chief advisors on finance. It was never determined who perpetrated this act against the Mongol Muslim bureaucrat, but his replacements in the role provided his successor, the Chinese Lu Shizhong, a platform to exercise his prejudices. He instituted severe penalties for breaking the imperial monopoly on the production of liquor, which had the effect of angering Mongols and Chinese alike. Lu characterized the Mongol ruling class as "idle" and proposed that they be forced to raise herds on government land and turn over 80 percent of their profits to the imperial treasury. Among his solutions to the dwindling income of the treasury was to print more of the paper money that was already spurring on inflation. Lu was eventually accused by his abundant enemies of embezzlement and was thrown out of office and executed. His successor, a Uyghur or Tibetan named Sengge, was likewise unable to set the imperial finances in order and swiftly became hated inside and outside of the imperial court. He was also executed.

The dilemma facing Mongol rule in China is clearly stated by the authors of the *History of the Yuan*. The book, which is part of the *Twenty-Four Histories of China*, compiled in 1370 by the Ming Bureau of History, condemns the Mongols for a plethora of shortcomings. Generally, Mongols were unsuited to govern China because they were barbarians. Barbarians might conquer from the back of a horse, but they could never govern China because Chinese civilization was far too sophisticated and complicated for the Mongols to comprehend. Even when they put Chinese in positions of authority, such as Lu Shizhong, they were bound to fail because the foreigners were ultimately in control.

Kublai's troubles with religious disputes, the expression of ethnic and religious differences, and his failure to succeed in conquering Japan were compounded with his failure to force the capitulation of Southeast Asia. The great khan sent a letter to Vietnamese Emperor Trần Thánh Tông, demanding that he send treasure, scholars, doctors, astronomers, and other skilled workers, who Kublai would assimilate into the Mongol administration. Behind this was the Kublai's belief that the Vietnamese would supply troops for his continuing war against the Southern Song. This didn't happen, and Thánh Tông successfully postponed any visit he was commanded to make to Beijing. In fact, both he and his son succeeded in fending off Kublai's overtures to submit and his efforts to create a regime change in Vietnam. The final Mongol failure in Annam came with the success of General Trần Hưng Đạo in destroying a Mongol invasion fleet in 1285 and forcing ground troops out of his nation.

In the case of the annexation of Burma, the Mongols fared no better than they had in Vietnam. King Narathihapate, a colorful, bombastic despot, who was characterized by Marco Polo as a "puissant prince," dealt with the Mongol threat by testing the borders of his kingdom through attacking Mongol dependencies on the northern frontier. Having roundly wrested them from Mongol control, Narathihapate declined to figure out how to fend off the inevitable Mongol attack. Instead, he used the royal treasury and national manpower to build an enormous new temple, the Mingalezedi Pagoda, which may have been an effort to curry divine favor in the inevitable Mongol invasion. Narathihapate, however, was sorely mistaken for in 1277, the Mongols attacked under the leadership of the recently appointed governor of Yunnan, Nasir al-Din, the son of the highly competent Sayyid al-Din. Riding at breakneck speed down the mountains of Yunnan, the Mongol forces entered a land that Marco Polo said was full of "great woods abounding in elephants and unicorns and numbers of other wild beasts." When the forces of Nasir and King Narathihapate met, the Mongols faced an army unlike anything they had ever seen before. Burmese archers loosed volleys of arrows down from their elevated howdahs. The Mongol horsemen were unable to approach the phalanx of elephants as their horses took fright at the daunting animals. Hiding in a forest, Nasir's archers dismounted and shot shafts into the charging elephants, forcing Narathihapate's army to retreat. The king was forced to take poison by one of his sons, who was aghast at his father's loss of the capital and his commencement of negotiations to submit to Mongol rule. One of Narathihapate's sons attempted to claim the kingship and agreed to submit to the Mongols, but the kingdom was in disarray, with several factions vying for power. This complicated the Mongol cause as they were used to dealing with a single monarch, and making peace with a dubious pretender to the throne did not suit their cause. In effect, if the Mongols were to take Burma, they would have to wage war all over the country and subdue the rebellious viceroys one by one. A Mongol invasion in 1287 failed to subdue the disunified country, and in 1303, the Mongols finally left Burma to its own devices.

By 1280, though, Kublai was a sick man. He was overweight and crippled with gout, with both conditions being brought on by long-term overconsumption of alcohol. Marco Polo reported that the great khan traveled in a great wooden bastion "borne by four well-trained elephants, and over him was hoisted his standard." The traveling bastion was put to use when Kublai had to deal with a revolt in Manchuria, where another grandson of Genghis Khan, Nayan, claimed that Kublai had strayed too far from his Mongol roots. Kublai himself led a flotilla in 1287, and when his warriors disembarked, he led his massive army against Nayan. The great khan's entourage was "full of cross-bow men and archers," and he rode under his banner, "bearing the figures of the sun and moon." According to Marco Polo, the great khan's four elephants "were covered with very stout boiled hides, overlaid with cloths of silk and gold." Nayan, a Nestorian Christian, was defeated and executed.

Despite his failing health, Kublai continued his expansionist campaigns. An emissary to the Kingdom of Java in 1289 had his face branded and was summarily extradited from the island. It took some time for the great khan to learn of this humiliation, but when he did, he set the traditional Mongol system of retribution in motion. As if a branded and expelled ambassador wasn't enough to rile the Mongol court in Beijing, Kertanagara, the king of Java (r. 1268–1292), attacked and defeated the Mongol vassal state of Jumbi in Sumatra.

In 1292, a fleet sailed from China under orders to return Jumbi to Mongol control, defeat the Javanese, and turn the Kingdom of Java into a Mongol vassal state. As part of this flotilla was a group of ships that peeled away to India. It is supposed that on board one of these vessels was Marco Polo, who was delivering a Mongol princess bride to the Ilkhanate in Persia. Before the Mongols reached Java, Kertanagara was killed by one of his allies, and the dead king's son turned to the Mongols for assistance in avenging the death of his father. The rebel ally of the king of Java was defeated and killed, whereupon the dead king's son turned on his saviors, the Mongols, and declared his independence. Unwilling and unable to turn Java into a vassal state, the Mongol flotilla returned to China.

Early in 1294, the nearly eighty-year-old, obese, alcoholic Kublai died. In spite of his physical condition, he had done pretty well to have achieved this age. He was succeeded by his grandson, Temür, who served as the next great khan of the Mongol Empire until 1307. Under Temür, the Pagan Kingdom (Burma), the Tran Kingdom of Annam, and all southern Vietnam accepted the supremacy of the Mongols.

In the writing of history, much significance has been put on the travels of Marco Polo and his father and uncle. They were, in fact, not the initiators of European trade along the Silk Road. Before their trip and residence in Kublai's court, the route had been exploited by merchants from the Latin West. Determining exactly what this trade involved is difficult because the details of commercial enterprises by Europeans in the East were guarded as secrets by traders, who, in order to protect their advantage, kept their affairs private. When the Polos returned to Venice in 1295, their Italian compatriots had established trading businesses around the Black Sea, and the Genoese had established commercial activities in Persia. It was reported that around nine hundred Genoese were residents of Persia in the service of Arghun Khan, principally constructing galleys for Mongol trade in the Indian Ocean. European trade with Persia expanded when the pope forbade trade with the Mamluks of Egypt in the early 14th century. Venetian merchants also expanded their trade with the Persians during this time, setting up a consulate in Tabriz and establishing Dominican and Franciscan convents there. At the same time, Italian traders based in ports in the Black Sea penetrated central Asia, dealing in goods brought from China and India. It is recorded that in 1291, Peter of Lucalongo, who was perhaps a Venetian merchant, traveled from the Near East to southern China. In 1305, letters were sent to the West by a Latin missionary, reporting that a colony of Genoese and other Italian merchants had established depots at Zaiton on the Straits of Formosa. At the same time as the Europeans were exploring and trading along the Silk Road, they were developing trade by sea from China.

By the middle of the 14th century, the route along the Silk Road that was followed by the Polos was fairly well-known among Latin merchants. In the *Book of Descriptions of Countries and of Measures Employed in Business*, which was written by a Florentine trader, Francesco Balducci Pegolotti, in about 1343, the author said that the road from Persia to China "is quite safe both by day and by night." But, he warns, if a trader is on the road when the overlord dies, "in the interval sometimes a disorder occurs against the Franks and other foreigners—they call 'Franks' all Christians of countries from the Byzantine Empire westwards—and the road is not safe until the new lord is sent for who is to reign after the one who died."

This was a bit of deception, as it was based on second-hand knowledge. In fact, traveling the Silk Road was a daunting affair. The challenges of the central Asia steppes, deserts, and mountains were, however, worth the effort for traders who acquired ginger, sugar, and rhubarb, items which were all prized in Europe as much as silk. The most sought-after silk was that produced in Turkestan. That overland trade with China was extensive by the mid-14th century is indicated by the discovery of two Christian tombstones in Yangzhou (in China's Jiangsu province). They are dated in Gothic lettering and are for the children of a Genoese merchant who died in 1342 and 1344. Trade must have been settled enough for Latin merchants to bring along family members as they were setting up businesses in China.

Conclusion: The Decline of Trade Along the Silk Road

After the death of Kublai Khan in 1294, the Mongol Empire, which included Yuan China, was led by his grandson, Temür Khan. He maintained Mongol policies and worked to discharge the debts of his father for military campaigns, particularly those against Vietnam. Temür also appointed court officials from among several ethnic groups and religions, including individuals of Tibetan and Khwarezmian origins. Although Confucianism was the court religion, officials included Muslims, Buddhists, Taoists, and Christians. He established peace with breakaway khanates, including bringing the Golden Horde in the West under his control. Temür Khan ended Mongol expansion in the south and east, ceasing to demand the complete submission of Japan, Burma, and Đại Việt (Vietnam).

Despite Temür Khan's reforms, his reign marks the beginning of the slow collapse of the Mongol-led Yuan dynasty in China and the larger Mongol Empire as a whole. A number of factors played a role in this. The small number of Mongols in the administration of vassal states allowed unrest to grow unchecked. These rebellious leaders of various ethnicities, situated anywhere from China to the

Near East, fractured the Mongol Empire, resulting in the formation of independent states that were freed from their subservience to the central government in Beijing. The rise of non-Mongol states along the Silk Road made travel and navigating complex and different trade regulations extremely difficult. In China itself, the remnants of the Mongol ruling class were forced to retreat to their traditional homeland, where their society had devolved into the kind of quasi-feudalism similar to that under Genghis Khan.

The last of the Mongol emperors of China, Toghon Temür Khan (r. 1333-1368) was a dissolute character, much like Roman Emperor Caligula. He preferred sexual orgies to administration, and so, the split between the four parts of the Mongol Empire—China (with Mongolia, Korea, and Tibet), central Asia, the Ilkhanate in western Asia, and the Golden Horde in Russia—became permanent.

What was to become the most powerful empire in the years of lessening Mongol control was founded in Turco-Mongol Persia by Timur or Tamerlane (r. 1370-1405) in Iran and central Asia. Timur's ethnicity was distinctly not Mongol, but he fashioned himself as a warlord in the tradition of Genghis Khan. His military successes in Persia, central Asia, India, Armenia, Georgia, and Syria indicate that he had the military ability and the means to be a successful emulator of Genghis Khan. While Timur was expanding his empire in the West, in China, the first of the Ming emperors were ridding the country of the remnants of Yuan loyalists. In 1394, the Ming emperor was in a position where he could write boldly to Timur, making the claim that Timur himself was subject to Ming authority. After making an alliance with the Mongols living in Mongolia, Timur prepared to attack Ming China. Before reaching the border of China, he died. His body was embalmed and taken back to Samarkand to be interred in a tomb, known as the Gur-e Amir, which still stands today.

The interruption of the land trade route from China to the West by the rise of Timur in the 14th century was more than made up for by the expansion in maritime trade between the East and West. Seaborne exploration and trade in China date back to the creation of a navy in the period of the Qin dynasty (221–206 BCE), and based on the excavation of a shipyard in Guangzhou, maritime activity was quite sophisticated in the early Han dynasty (201 BCE–220 CE). The coastline of the South China Sea seems to have been the extent of early Chinese seaborne trade. Chinese merchants sailed into the Indian Ocean from the late 2nd century BCE and are said to have traveled as far as Ethiopia. Travel to and from India was commonplace by the 7th century, as Chinese vessels would often sail to the Red Sea and up the Euphrates River in modern-day Iraq.

Chinese seaborne mercantilism changed in the 15th century during the period of the explorations of Zheng He, who led seven expeditions into the Indian Ocean under orders from the Yongle Emperor, the third emperor of the Ming Dynasty. Zheng He's voyages were aboard ships that were larger than had ever been constructed in China. Some of his vessels, which were made to carry treasure back to China, may have measured as much as 400 feet long and 170 feet wide. On his first voyage, which lasted from 1405 to 1407, Zheng He reached Calcutta. In subsequent journeys, he explored as far as the coast of Africa. The strange things he brought back to China—animals, art, and manufactured goods—provided the impetus for the growth of vast maritime trading enterprises.

In the wake of Zheng He's voyages, the East/West maritime trade between China, Indochina, India, Africa, and Persia expanded to such an extent that it replaced the arduous land route of the Silk Road. Shortly after Zheng He explored maritime routes to the West, Europeans, principally Spanish and Portuguese explorers, set out to discover maritime routes to the East, where they knew goods sought after in European markets could be obtained. The Portuguese sailor Bartolomeu Dias, who lived from 1450 to 1500, reached the Cape of Good Hope and determined that the east coast of Africa was accessible by ship. He was followed by Vasco da

Gama, who lived from around 1460 to 1524 and who rounded the tip of Africa and reached India. By opening up maritime trade to the East, the Europeans were able to dispense with the services of Arab intermediaries. This led to the opening up of longer trade routes to the Far East, including China and the Pacific Islands.

It was in the Age of Discovery (the early 15th century to the mid-17th century) that alternative trade routes between the East and the West replaced the Silk Road. The transporting of goods by sea was much cheaper and quicker than overland transport. Larger quantities of goods could also be moved with greater reliability, as they were subject only to the dangers of the sea, which were minimal compared to the dangers of marauders and greedy upstart ethnic regimes that infested the Silk Road. The old Silk Road did not fall into complete disuse as the traditional intercommunity trade continues to exist up to the present day.

Here's another book by Captivating History that you might like

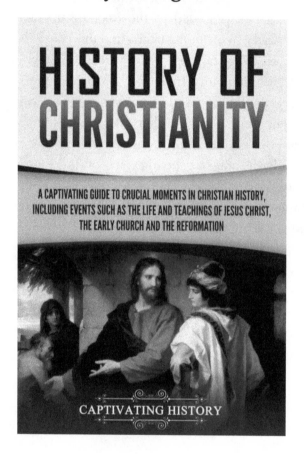

Free Bonus from Captivating History
(Available for a Limited time)

Hi History Lovers!

Now you have a chance to join our exclusive history list so you can get your first history ebook for free as well as discounts and a potential to get more history books for free! Simply visit the link below to join.

Captivatinghistory.com/ebook

Also, make sure to follow us on Facebook, Twitter and Youtube by searching for Captivating History.

Further Reading

Christopher Beckwith, *Empires of the Silk Road: A History of Central Eurasia from the Bronze Age to the Present* (Princeton: Princeton University Press, 2009)

Peter Hopkirk, *Foreign Devils on the Silk Road: The Search for the Lost Cities and Treasures of Chinese Central Asia* (London: Murray, 1980)

John Man, *Genghis Khan: Life, Death and Resurrection* (New York: Thomas Dunne Books, 2004)

Jonathan Clements, *A Brief History of Khublai Khan: Lord of Xanadu, Emperor of China* (London: Robinson, 2010).

Jaroslav Folda, *Crusader Art: The Art of the Crusaders in the Holy Land, 1099-1291* (Aldershot and Burlington: Lund Humphries, 2008)

Thomas F. Madden, *A Concise History of the Crusades.* (Lanham: Maryland: Rowman & Littlefield, 2013)

Steven Runciman, *A History of the Crusades.* (Cambridge: University Press, 1954)

Rodney Stark, *God's Battalions*, (NY: HarperOne, 2009)

Christopher Tyerman, *God's War: A New History of the Crusades.* (Harvard University Press, 2006